The Rhetorical Composition
and Function of Hebrews 11

The Rhetorical Composition and Function of Hebrews 11

In Light of Example Lists in Antiquity

Michael R. Cosby

MERCER

ISBN 0-86554-320-8

BS
2775.2
.C67
1988

The paper used in this publication meets
the minimum requirements of American National Standard
for Information Sciences—Permanence of Paper
for Printed Library Materials, ANSI Z39.48-1984.

Library of Congress Cataloging-in-Publication Data

The rhetorical composition and function of hebrews 11 :
in light of example lists in antiquity / Michael R. Cosby.
xii + 132 pages   6x9″ (15x23cm.)
Bibliography: p. 111
Includes index.
ISBN 0-86554-320-8 (alk. paper)
1. Bible. N.T. Hebrews XI—Criticism, interpretation, etc.
I. Title.
BS2775.2.C67   1988   88-27570
227′.87066—dc19   CIP

Contents

Preface

Research takes many unexpected twists and turns as one confronts and grapples with new and unforeseen data. This book represents one of those unexpected trajectories, for the scope of this study changed substantially from what I initially envisioned.

I had set out to prove that Hebrews 11 represents a literary form, but after much digging through the multitude of ancient texts available, I concluded that my initial direction needed correction. Time will tell whether or not I am right in this conclusion, but the change in course proved to be extremely productive for my own research. Instead of working with literary forms, I found myself immersed in the ancient rhetorical handbooks, seeking to understand how their authors described the fine art of persuasive communication.

The results were fascinating. A whole new vista opened up, and I began to read aloud the Greek text before me to *hear* the *sounds* of effective argumentation. Instead of looking primarily for logical development of ideas, I began to hear the efforts to make arguments *sound* persuasive. My failure to find a form became my initiation into a new world of orality, the world of the ancient rhetorician. What began as disappointment became the joy of discovery.

The Loeb Classical Library was an indispensable resource for investigating the ancient world of rhetoric, and I use numerous quotations from this series in my study. I wish to thank Harvard University Press for granting permission to reprint this material.

Because this book represents a substantial reduction and revision of my dissertation, I am extremely grateful to Arthur W. Wainwright, mentor and friend, for his insight and encouragement as my dissertation director. I also thank William L. Lane for his careful reading of the manuscript and many suggestions for improvement. Most of all I thank my wife, Lynne, for her loving support and hours of help. But I dedicate the work to my son, Allen, whose premature birth and difficult start in life added to the stress of writing a dissertation. He has overcome the obstacles and flourishes before me as a wonderful reminder that difficult beginnings sometimes lead to greatly appreciated endings.

Michael R. Cosby
August 1988

Abbreviations

AT   Author's translation.

BibZeit   *Biblische Zeitschrift.*

Bleek   Friedrich Bleek, *Der Brief an die Hebräer* (Berlin: Ferdinand Dümmler, 1840).

Bruce   F. F. Bruce, *The Epistle to the Hebrews,* NICNT (Grand Rapids: Eerdmans, 1964).

Buchanan   George Wesley Buchanan, *To the Hebrews,* Anchor Bible 36 (Garden City NY: Doubleday, 1972).

Calvin   John Calvin, *Commentaries on the Epistle of Paul the Apostle to the Hebrews,* trans. J. Owen (Grand Rapids: Eerdmans, 1948).

CBQ   *Catholic Biblical Quarterly.*

CBQMS   Catholic Biblical Quarterly Monograph Series.

CD   Damascus Document.

Delitzsch   Franz Delitzsch, *Commentary on the Epistle to the Hebrews,* 2 vols., Clark's Foreign Theological Library 25, trans. T. L. Kingsbury (Edinburgh: T.&T. Clark, 1870).

Gouge   William Gouge, *Commentary on Hebrews* (Edinburgh: J. Nichol, 1866; rpt.: Grand Rapids: Kregel Publications, 1980).

Héring   Jean Héring, *The Epistle to the Hebrews*, trans. A. W. Heathcote and P. J. Allcock (London: Epworth Press, 1970).

ICC   International Critical Commentary.

JBL   *Journal of Biblical Literature.*

JSOT   *Journal for the Study of the Old Testament.*

Lausberg   Heinrich Lausberg, *Handbuch der literarischen Rhetorik: Eine Grundlegung der Literaturwissenschaft,* 2 vols. (München: Max Hueber, 1960).

LXX   The Septuagint.

LCL   The Loeb Classical Library.

Martin   Josef Martin, *Antike Rhetorik: Technik und Methode,* Handbuch der Altertumswissenschaft (München: C. H. Beck, 1974).

Michel   Otto Michel, *Der Brief an die Hebräer,* 13 Auflage, Meyer Kommentar (Göttingen: Vandenhoeck & Ruprecht, 1975).

Moffatt   James Moffatt, *A Critical and Exegetical Commentary on the Epistle to the Hebrews,* ICC (New York: Charles Scribner's Sons, 1924).

Montefiore Hugh Montefiore, *A Commentary on the Epistle to the Hebrews,* Harper's NT Commentaries (New York: Harper & Row, 1964).

NICNT   New International Commentary on the New Testament, ed. F. F. Bruce.

NIDNTTh   New International Dictionary of New Testament Theology, ed. Colin Brown.

NIV   New International Version, 1973.

NovT   *Novum Testamentum.*

NT   New Testament.

NTS   *New Testament Studies.*

OT   Old Testament.

Owen   John Owen, *An Exposition of the Epistle to the Hebrews,* vol. 7
          (New York: Robert Carter & Brothers, 1855).

RevExp   *Review and Expositor.*

RSV   Revised Standard Version, ²1971, ¹1946.

SBL   Society of Biblical Literature.

Spicq   C. Spicq, *L'Épître aux Hébreux,* 2 vols., Études Bibliques (Paris:
          Librairie Lecoffre, 1953).

Stuart   Moses Stuart, *A Commentary on the Epistle to the Hebrews,* 2nd
          ed. (New York: J. Leavitt, 1833).

TDNT   *Theological Dictionary of the New Testament,* 9 vols., ed. Gerhard
          Kittel and Gerhard Friedrich, trans. Geoffrey W. Bromiley (Grand
          Rapids MI: Eerdmans, 1964–1974).

Tholuck   A. Tholuck, *A Commentary on the Epistle to the Hebrews,* 2 vols.,
          The Biblical Cabinet 39, trans. J. Hamilton (Edinburgh: Thomas
          Clark, 1842).

Vanhoye   Albert Vanhoye, *La Structure Littéraire de L'Épître aux Hébreux,*
          Studia Neotestamentica 1 (Paris: Desclée De Brouwer, 1963).

Westcott B. F. Westcott, *The Epistle to the Hebrews* (London: Macmillan,
          1909).

Windisch Hans Windisch, *Der Hebräerbrief,* zweite Auflage, Handbuch zum
          Neuen Testament 14 (Tübingen: J. C. B. Mohr, 1931).

ZNW   *Zeitschrift für die neutestamentliche Wissenschaft.*

Dedication

To
Allen Michael Cosby
my firstborn
my gift from God

Chapter 1

Hebrews 11 and Ancient Rhetoric

Introduction

Although no one today knows the identity of the author of Hebrews, many recognize and appreciate his[1] rhetorical ability. His Greek is among the best in the New Testament, and the persuasive power with which he writes is extremely well documented. B. F. Westcott declares that

> the language of the Epistle is both in vocabulary and style purer and more vigorous than that of any other book in the N.T. The vocabulary is singularly copious . . . [and studying it] will illustrate the freedom and power with which the author of the Epistle dealt with the resources of the Greek language. . . . The style is even more characteristic of a practiced scholar than the vocabulary. It would be difficult to find anywhere passages more exact and pregnant in expression than i. 1-4; ii. 14-18; vii. 26-28; xii. 18-24. The language, the order, the rhythm, the parenthetical involutions, all contribute to the total effect. The writing shows everywhere traces of effort and care. . . . The author . . . has, like an artist, simply to give life

---

[1]Some have argued that Hebrews was written by a woman, but this is very much a minority position, and I will use masculine pronouns throughout to designate the author. For arguments that Priscilla wrote Hebrews, see Adolf Harnack, ''Probabilia über die Adresse und den Verfasser des Hebräerbriefs,'' *ZNW* 1 (1900): 16-41; and Ruth Hoppin, *Priscilla, Author of the Epistle to the Hebrews* (New York: Exposition Press, 1969).

to the model which he has already completely fashioned. This is true even of the noblest rhetorical passages, such as c. xi.[2]

Adolf Deissmann states that Hebrews "is historically the earliest example of Christian artistic literature. . . . [T] his epistle strives to rise above the stratum in which Christianity had its origin towards the higher level of learning and culture."[3] Paul Wendland places Hebrews in a literary class by itself among other New Testament documents.[4] And James W. Thompson calls attention to the "extraordinarily sophisticated Greek style throughout" and asserts that "It is thus undisputed that Hebrews is a unique form of early Christian literature."[5]

With power and authority the author of Hebrews speaks to his audience, seeking to convince this discouraged group of Christians not to turn away from their Christian faith. Knowing that some of them are ready to give up prompts him to employ an impressive set of persuasive techniques in which he shows himself to be well acquainted with ancient rhetorical devices.[6] Probably the most rhetorical section in his homily,[7] however, is

---

[2]Westcott, xliv, xlv-xlvi. Note also the praise given by C. Spicq:

> Dialecticien et rhétoricien consommé, l'auteur de *Hébr.* est bien loin de l'art décadent de la sophistique contemporaine, où l'exposé de la vérité est secondaire par rapport à la subtilité de la pensée, au cliquetis des syllabes, à sonorité des mots, à la forme piquante des expressions; on ne trouve chez lui à peu près acun de ces lieux connuns dont les orateurs et les écrivains de l'époque faisaient un si large usage. S'il abonde en finesses littéraires, elles ne sont jamais artificielles; la profondeur et la rigueur des idées l'emportent sur les raffinements du style; celui-ci est l'expression toujours heureuse de celles-là; l'art n'intervient que pour donner à la pensée une force et une séduction plus vives. (1:365-66)

[3]Adolf Deissmann, *Light from the Ancient East,* trans. L. R. M. Strachan (New York: Doran, 1927) 244.

[4]P. Wendland, *Die urchristlichen Literaturformen* (Tübingen: Mohr, 1912) 307; see also E. Norden, *Agnostos Theos* (Darmstadt: Wissenschaftliche Buchgesellschaft, 5. Auflage, 1971) 386.

[5]J. W. Thompson, *The Beginnings of Christian Philosophy: The Epistle to the Hebrews,* CBMS 13 (Washington DC: The Catholic Biblical Association of America, 1982) 1.

his list of heroes of the faith in chapter 11. Each of the eighteen examples employed in 11:3-31 begins with πίστει ("By faith"). This repetition of an initial word, called "anaphora" by ancient rhetoricians,[8] is so pronounced that few commentators fail to mention it. C. Spicq pointedly remarks, "By its repetition of πίστει, πίστει, πίστει at the beginning of successive statements, chapter 11 provides the best example of anaphora in the entire Bible and perhaps in all of profane literature as well."[9] Ironically, however, scholars have failed to notice that there are a number of other rhetorical techniques employed in Hebrews 11 that complement and strengthen the more obvious anaphora.[10]

In a highly efficient manner the author implements this series of rhetorical techniques in Hebrews 11 to persuade his audience to stand firm in their Christian commitment. These people had experienced persecution

---

[6]Spicq in particular provides a summary of the linguistic and literary characteristics in 1: 351-78. On 358-66 he treats the rhetorical language used in Hebrews.

[7]In spite of considerable disagreement over the life setting of Hebrews, there is a concensus among modern scholars that it is a homily. See Harwig Thyen, *Der Stil Der Jüdisch-Hellenistichen Homilie,* Forschungen zur Religion und Literatur des Alten und Neuen Testaments (Göttingen: Vandenhoeck & Ruprecht, 1955) 16-18; James Swetnam, "On the Literary Genre of the 'Epistle' to the Hebrews," *NovT* 11 (1969) 261; J. C. McCullough, "Some Recent Developments in Research on the Epistle to the Hebrews," *Irish Biblical Studies* 2 (1980): 152-53.

[8]See *Rhetorica ad Herennium* IV.19-20 for a good description of anaphora. Also see Lausberg, 227-34; and A. Baumstark, "Anaphora" in *Reallexikon für Antike und Christentum,* vol.1, ed. Theodore Klauser (Stuttgart: Hiersemann, 1950) 418-27.

[9]Spicq, 1: 362 (AT).

[10]Much careful work has been devoted to determining the literary structure of Hebrews, the most thorough of which is Albert Vanhoye's *La structure littéraire de l'épître aux Hébreux* (see 183-95 for Hebrews 11). Also see Vanhoye, "Discussions sur la structure de l'Épître aux Hébreux," *Biblica* 55 (1974): 349-80; James Swetnam, "Form and Content in Hebrews 1-6," *Biblica* 53 (1972): 368-85; and "Form and Content in Hebrews 7-13," *Biblica* 55 (1974): 333-48; Jukka Thurén, *Das Lobopfer der Hebräer,* Studien zum Aufbau und Anliegen von Hebräerbrief 13 (Acta Academiae Aboensis, Ser. A, vol. 47 nr. 1; Åbo 1973); R. Gyllenberg, "Die Komposition des Hebräerbriefs," *Svensk Exegetisk Årsbok* 22-23 (1957-58): 137-47; L. Vaganay, "Le plan de l'Épître aux Hébreux," in *Memorial Lagrange,* ed. L.-H. Vincent (Paris, 1940) 269-77.

(10:32-34; 12:3-4), and some of them were so discouraged that they had begun to avoid the Christian assemblies (2:1-3; 10:25; compare 3:6, 14; 12:3, 12). During their earlier days as Christians, they had joyfully endured persecution because of their belief in the trustworthiness of the proclamation (10:34), but now they have become dubious about the wisdom of taking such a strong Christian stance that they experience opposition (10:35). Theirs is a crisis of faith, a crisis felt by many down through the centuries for similar or very different reasons, a crisis of wondering whether or not their Christian beliefs are true and merit living for an unseen future reward.

To inspire a tenacious faith in these faltering believers, the author of Hebrews sends a sermon; and in chapter 11 he provides a list of examples of past believers who remained loyal to God in spite of opposition. Carefully he constructs this list to make the people in it appear to represent many other faithful men and women of God who could also be cited from salvation history. Each of these heroes illustrates that from the dawn of human history to the present day God has called his people to a life of self-sacrificing faith.

This list is, therefore, far from a mere presentation of data. The author composes it in such a way as to *sound* persuasive to his audience. He relies heavily on artistic use of language, on implementation of rhetorical techniques that greatly enhance the effectiveness of his message. The forcefulness of his words is therefore somewhat diminished if one does not *hear* the convincing sound of his message.

The Oral Nature of Ancient Writing

One may only speculate on the educational background of the author of Hebrews. He may have received formal training in one of the schools in Alexandria, but this is merely a guess. What can be asserted is that, even from the first sentence of Hebrews, the author's ability to use artistically crafted language is readily apparent.

Πολυμερῶς καὶ πολυτρόπως πάλαι . . .
In many ways and various ways long ago. . . .

Such use of paronomasia (word play) characterizes his rhetorical selection of words in an effort to strengthen his message further by making it *sound* convincing.

Although scholars have for some time recognized that ancient writers produced their works to be heard,[11] this knowledge has been slow to exercise a significant influence on biblical studies. Some biblical scholars are employing the findings of people like Milman Parry, A. B. Lord, Eric A. Havelock, Walter Ong, and others[12] on the differences between primarily oral and primarily literate societies.[13] Such efforts show promise and will necessitate the rethinking of some accepted concepts in biblical studies. Work is also progressing in the area of classical rhetoric, which bears more directly on the present study.[14] In highly rhetorical texts like Hebrews 11, comprehension of the intended message of ancient authors is enhanced considerably when one seeks not only to *see* their words printed on a page but also to *hear* these words. There is an element of persuasiveness and understanding available only through *listening* to the text in its original language. Only through hearing the plays on the sounds of words and other orally based techniques can one fully appreciate the artistic compositions of these authors.

---

[11]See Josef Balogh, ''Voces Paginarum,'' *Philologus* 84 (1927): 84-109 and 202-40.

[12]For a helpful bibliography on these resources, see Walter Ong, *Orality and Literacy: The Technologizing of the Word* (New York: Methuen, 1982) 180-95.

[13]See the Bibliography in Werner Kelber, *The Oral and the Written Gospel: The Hermeneutics of Speaking and Writing in the Synoptic Tradition, Mark, Paul and Q* (Philadelphia: Fortress Press, 1983).

[14]For example, see George A. Kennedy, *New Testament Interpretation through Rhetorical Criticism* (Chapel Hill: The University of North Carolina Press, 1984). A number of works on rhetoric analyze NT documents more on a macro level, seeking to show that they conform to the prescribed sequences of ancient speeches. Dieter Betz divides Galatians into Epistolary Prescript (1:1-5), *Exordium* (1:6-11), *Narratio* (1:12-2:14), *Propositio* (2:15-21), *Probatio* (3:1-4:31), *Exhortatio* (5:1-6:10), and Epistolary Postscript or *Conclusio* (6:11-18) (*Galatians,* Hermeneia [Philadelphia: Fortress Press, 1979] 14-25). James Swetnam (''Form and Content in Hebrews 1-6,'' *Biblica* 53 [1972]: 368-85; and ''Form and Content in Hebrews 7-13,'' *Biblica* 55 [1974]: 338-48) presents the following divisions for Hebrews: *Exordium* (1:1-4), Exposition (1:5-2:18); Exhortation (3:1-6:20), Exposition (7:1-10:18), Exhortation (10:19-39), Exposition-Exhortation (11:1-13:21). Such works provide important background for my study of Hebrews 11, but for the most part they address different issues.

Ancient texts were written to be heard partly because of the limited number of written texts in pre-printing-press societies. Jehoshua Gitay comments that

> even if a class of educated people knew how to read, the majority did not share this knowledge and, not less important, copies of written material in the pre-printing period were limited in number for physical reasons. Hence, the material had to be distributed orally in order to reach a wide audience.[15]

There was also the dimension of the *way* people read. George Kennedy observes regarding ancient Greek writing, "All literature was written to be heard, and even when reading to himself a Greek read aloud."[16] Late in the fourth century C.E., Augustine expresses shock over viewing Ambrose reading silently, without pronouncing the words as he read (*Confessions* VI.3).[17] Silent reading, the norm today in Western cultures, was extremely rare until well after the invention of the printing press.[18] Ancient authors wrote their works to be heard, and in this predominantly oral world they considered rhetorical techniques as important in persuading an audience as the evidence presented in their argument.[19]

Kennedy explains that although Romans tended to neglect training in athletics, music, and other liberal arts, they considered training in speech to be essential. "The world was a rhetorician's world, its ideal an orator;

---

[15]Gitay, "Deutero-Isaiah: Oral or Written?" *JBL* 99 (1980): 191.

[16]Kennedy, *The Art of Persuasion in Greece* (Princeton: Princeton University Press, 1963) 4.

[17]H. J. Chaytor, *From Script to Print* (Cambridge: Cambridge University Press, 1945) esp. 13-21, for additional information on this topic.

[18]See John G. Bayer, "Narrative techniques and oral tradition in *The Scarlet Letter*," *American Literature* 52 (1980): 250-63; Ruth Crosby, "Oral Delivery in the Middle Ages," *Speculum* 11 (1936): 88-110; Moses Hadas, *Ancilla to Classical Reading* (New York: Columbia University Press, 1954); William Nelson, "From 'Listen, Lordings' to 'Dear Reader,'" *University of Toronto Quarterly* 46 (1976-77): 111-24; Walter Ong, *Rhetoric, Romance, and Technology* (Ithaca: Cornell University Press, 1971); and Ong, *Orality and Literacy*, 93-96, 117-23, 157-60.

[19]Kennedy, *New Testament Interpretation through Rhetoric*, 3.

speech became an artistic product to be admired apart from its content or significance."[20] H. I. Marrou calls rhetoric the queen of subjects for students in the Hellenistic age and points out that "for the very great majority of students, higher education meant taking lessons from the rhetor, learning the art of eloquence from him."[21] Obtaining such education was not difficult, for "rhetors were everywhere, in every self-respecting city."[22]

Even many of the philosophers who condemned the Sophists for their manipulative use of rhetoric clearly understood the need to master persuasive speaking techniques. Aristotle emphasizes the necessity of good delivery (ὑπόκρισις) in a speech, for mere presentation of the facts may not convince people: "It is not sufficient to know what one ought to say, but one must also know how to say it" (*Rhetoric* III.1.2).[23] He states that "since the whole business of Rhetoric is to influence opinion, we must pay attention to it [ὑπόκρισις], not as being right, but necessary . . . owing to the corruption of the hearer" (III.1.5).[24] Although Aristotle did not believe that style and manner of delivery were of importance to the serious student, he recognized their influence in the persuasion of others and therefore considered them necessary to master (III.1.6).[25]

---

[20]Kennedy, *The Art of Persuasion in Greece,* 22.

[21]Henri-I. Marrou, *A History of Education in Antiquity,* trans. G. Lamb (London: Sheed and Ward, 1956) 194.

[22]Ibid., 197.

[23]Trans. by John H. Freese, *Aristotle: The "Art" of Rhetoric,* LCL (New York: G. P. Putnam's Sons, 1926) 345. Compare Quintilian, *Inst. Orat.* IX.4.129-30 on the different rhythms used in different genres of speech.

[24]*Aristotle: The "Art" of Rhetoric,* 197. Aristotle explains that different styles of speaking work best before different audiences. In front of a larger crowd an overly refined speech can be disadvantageous, whereas before a single judge a lot of rhetorical devices and a loud voice are problematic (III.12.15). One should address a crowd with a less refined presentation, for they are more persuaded by the acting involved in the use of rhetorical techniques and less able to follow a detailed argument. Before a single judge, however, a logically developed argument spoken with grammatically refined language is more cogent.

[25]See also Longinus, *On The Sublime,* for numerous examples of effective use of language in order to grip an audience.

As an educated man of the first century C.E., the author of Hebrews mastered these rhetorical techniques. Therefore, to appreciate fully the scope of his argumentation, especially in passages like chapter 11, one must consider his rhetoric.

Hebrews 11 and Form Criticism

Demonstrating that the author of Hebrews consistently used rhetorical techniques is simple enough, but what was his source of inspiration for the list of examples of faithful persons in chapter 11? Did he employ a recognized literary or rhetorical form[26] that had proven itself to be effective, or did he compose the list extemporaneously as he considered the particular needs of those he addressed? Neither classical nor biblical scholars have yet determined whether the use of a list of heroes was a recognized rhetorical form in antiquity. And even if this question were answered in the affirmative, one would still face the problem of seeking to determine what influence the form exerted on the author.

Analysis of forms always involves the potential danger of violating the integrity of a particular text. James Muilenburg, who initiated the title "rhetorical criticism," warns against preoccupation with literary forms at the expense of specific texts, stating that

> form criticism by its very nature is bound to generalize because it is concerned with what is common to all the representatives of a genre, and therefore applies an external measure to the individual pericopes. It does not focus sufficient attention upon what is unique and unrepeatable, upon the particularity of the formulation. Moreover, form and content are inex-

---

[26]E.g., Windisch, 98: "Die literarische Form von Hebr 11." Such a form-critical investigation typically does not involve speculation on the oral prehistory of example lists but merely a determination of whether or not there are stereotyped features in many of these lists. "Form" in this case indicates a literary convention, such as H. Lausberg means when he says, "The *exemplum*, therefore, with regard to its source, has a *utilitas*-function and a literary form" (228, §410, AT). Cf. Martin J. Buss, "The Study of Forms," in *Old Testament Form Criticism*, ed. John H. Hayes (San Antonio TX: Trinity University Press, 1974) 54: "Form criticism has sometimes been described, especially in NT scholarship, as a study of the oral stage of the history of a literary text. However, there is no reason to limit form criticism to oral expressions; moreover, it is questionable whether an oral prehistory can be reconstructed in any detail on the basis of literary forms."

tricably related. They form an integral whole. The two are one. Exclusive attention to the *Gattung* may actually obscure the thought and intention of the writer or speaker. The passage must be read and heard precisely as it is spoken. It is the creative synthesis of the particular formulation of the pericope with the content that makes it the distinctive composition that it is.[27]

This does not mean, however, that Muilenburg saw no value in form-critical study. Appreciation of what he calls the "creative synthesis" of the common and the specific involves an investigation of the literary genre in question. By first understanding the kind of literature being studied, one can more accurately assess an author's creativity in a particular passage.[28]

The highly stylized composition of Hebrews 11 clearly sets it apart from its surrounding context. When compared to the style of Hebrews as a whole, its lengthy parade of famous people is quite distinct. Indeed, if the chapter were omitted entirely, the author's exhortation would still flow quite nicely. This fact has led some to conclude that the chapter was borrowed by the author from another source or that he employed a recognized homiletical form in his address. Among the claims that Hebrews 11 represents a particular form, however, are diverse opinions on how to define the form it represents. Hebrews 11 has been categorized with a number of different kinds of texts, sometimes on the basis of the mere fact that they list famous people, sometimes on the basis of compositional similarity, and occasionally on the basis of functional considerations.

Hans Windisch entitles a section in his commentary "Die literarische Form von Hebr 11" (The literary Form of Hebrews 11),[29] but only in a very cursory way does he compare it with other lists. On the basis of Wisdom 10, Sirach 44-50, 4 Maccabees 16:16-23, and Philo's *On the Virtues* 198ff. and *On Rewards and Punishments* 1ff., Windisch asserts that the author of Hebrews had a Jewish source for his tract of faith in chapter 11: "Up until ὀνειδισμὸς Χριστοῦ in v. 26 and the final observation in vv. 39-40, the entire passage could have been designed by a Jew. At the

---

[27]James Muilenburg, "Form Criticism and Beyond," *JBL* 88 (1969): 5.

[28]Ibid., 4-9

[29]Windisch, 98-99.

very least a Jewish or Jewish-Christian school tradition lies behind its present composition.''[30] Otto Michel largely follows Windisch but modifies his view somewhat by saying Hebrews 11 is based on a Jewish source (*Vorlage*) which probably consisted of verses 3-12, 17-31, and 32-38.[31] Michel adds 4 Ezra 7:105ff. to Windisch's list of parallels and says these texts represent an ''outspoken style of teaching'' (*ausgesprochenen Lehrstil*) which connected historical examples under a particular viewpoint.[32] He makes a distinction, however, between Acts 7, a historical outline with a distinct viewpoint, and the more highly formulated lists in Hebrews 11 and 1 Clement which employ catchwords to link together their examples.[33] Michel speculates that such linking together of examples was originally a Hellenistic rhetorical and homiletical technique, not a literary phenomenon. Therefore he calls Hebrews 11 an example of Jewish theology expressed with a Hellenistic form.

Along this line, Hartwig Thyen's work is important. Seeking to reconstruct the style of the synagogue homily in Hellenistic Judaism,[34] he comments on example lists (*Beispielreihen*) of people from Jewish history,[35] calling them a decidedly Hellenistic aspect of synagogue homilies. Thyen believes the lengthy summaries in Israel's history that show how God led his people (for example, Psalm 105:10-44), or that contrast God's faithfulness with Israel's disobedience (for example, Psalms 78; 106; Nehemiah 9:6-31),[36] were modified in the Diaspora from their focus on God's goal in history to an interest in the virtues of pious people. He attributes this

---

[30]Ibid. (AT).

[31]Michel, 371, 422-23. Cf. Gotfried Schille's extreme attempt to dissect Hebrews 11 into various sources in ''Katechese und Taufliturgie: Erwägungen zu Hebräerbrief 11,'' *ZNW* 51 (1960): 112-31.

[32]Michel, 371.

[33]Ibid.

[34]Thyen, *Der Stil*, 5.

[35]Ibid., 18, 49-50. Thyen agrees with Windisch that Hebrews 11 is based on a Jewish source (*Vorlage*).

[36]Ibid., 111. Thyen cites Wisdom 10; Sirach 44-50; Judith 5:6ff.; Acts 13:17ff.; and the series of images (*Bilderzyklus*) in the synagogue at Dura.

change largely to the propaganda efforts by such people as Philo's circle at Alexandria, who made universal symbols out of the heroes of Israel's history.[37] Hebrews 11 is therefore an instance of such a Hellenized list of examples strung together by means of a catchword.

C. Spicq provides a wealth of information with regard to the eulogizing of ancient worthies in Greco-Roman literature and the use of exemplary men or women in ancient rhetoric,[38] but his comparisons of Hebrews 11 with other lists are cursory and involve only Jewish and Christian texts. He does note functional differences between Hebrews 11 and other lists, however, interacting briefly with the purposes of Wisdom 10, Sirach 44-50 and 1 Maccabees 2:51-60.[39]

F. F. Bruce adds further clarification regarding Hebrews 11 and Sirach 44-50, saying that Sirach points out "all the commendable qualities of the men of God whom he commemorated," while the author of Hebrews "confines himself to those features of his heroes' careers which illustrate their faith in God."[40] He states that Mattathias's last speech in 1 Maccabees 2:51-60 is therefore a better parallel with Hebrews 11, for it stimulates zeal by recalling specifically the faithfulness under testing of certain biblical figures. Bruce also cites as parallels Wisdom 10; CD II.16ff.; 4 Maccabees 16:20ff.; 18:11ff., and 1 Clement 4:1ff.; 9:1ff.; 55:1ff., and asserts that

> the literary genre is by no means confined to the Judaeo-Christian tradition; it shares many characteristics with the *diatribe* of Stoic-influenced rhetoric, which was given to the accumulation of historical or legendary examples of the particular quality under discussion.[41]

---

[37]Ibid., 111-12

[38]Spicq 1:18-21

[39]Spicq 2:335. Spicq calls the listing of famous people a traditional literary theme in Judaism (cf. Philo, *On Rewards and Punishments* 1ff.) and early Christianity (Acts 7; Jas 5:10-11; 1 Clem. 4ff.; cf. Iren., *Against Heresies* II.30.9; Const. Apost. VIII.12). The faith or virtue of God's eminent representatives caused them to be used as examples for contemporary conduct. Like other authors, the author of Hebrews used the example list to give evidence for the true nature of faith (Spicq 2:335).

[40]Bruce, 279.

[41]Ibid., 280.

Bruce is only partially correct in this, however, for although Stoic diatribes do often employ examples to prove particular points, they rarely formulate example lists. His claim that these texts form a literary genre is somewhat misleading.

Von Armin Schmitt's "Struktur, Herkunft und Bedeutung der Beispielreihe in Weis 10" provides some interesting Greco-Roman lists of which the authors of works on Hebrews 11 do not mention: Homer, *Iliad* V.381-402; *Odyssey* V.118-120, 121-29; Isocrates, *Antidosis* 231-35, and Lycurgus, *Against Leocrates* 83-129.[42] But perhaps the most important study of the forms of ancient lists to date is Thomas R. Lee's dissertation, "Studies in the Form of Sirach (Ecclesiasticus) 44-50."[43] Lee classifies lists according to their compositional characteristics. Within the Hebrew canon he divides them into (1) hymns: Psalms 105; 135; 136; and (2) deuteronomistic surveys of history: Psalms 78; 106; Nehemiah 9; Ezekiel 20.[44] From texts outside the Hebrew canon he classifies (1) hymns: Judith 16:1-17; (2) deuteronomistic surveys of history: Judith 5:5-21; Acts 7:2-53; (3) example lists (*Beispielreihen*): 1 Maccabees 2:51-60; 3 Maccabees 2: 3-8; 6:2-8; 4 Maccabees 16:15-23; 18:9-19; Sirach 44-50; and Philo, *Every Good Man Is Free* 62-130, *On Rewards and Punishments* 67-78, *On the Virtues* 198-227; and (4) example lists formulated with catchwords: Wisdom 10; CD 2:17-3:2; Hebrews 11.[45]

In summary, whether or not the author of Hebrews used a rhetorical (homiletical) or literary form, or a Jewish source as the basis of chapter 11 is still a matter of debate. The number of example lists of famous people in the literature of antiquity that have been cited as parallels to Hebrews 11 is actually quite modest, and they are of sufficiently different composition and function that it is doubtful that their authors were following a set pattern when composing them. The fact that such lists were relatively unusual challenges the assumption that in the predominantly oral cultures of

---

[42]Schmitt, *BibZeit* 21 (1977): 1-22.

[43]T. R. Lee, "Studies in the Form of Sirach (Ecclesiasticus) 44-50" (Ph.D. diss., Graduate Theological Union, 1979).

[44]Ibid., 21-26.

[45]Ibid., 26-46.

antiquity the formulation of lists of famous individuals was widely seen as an effective rhetorical technique, and speakers merely modified this approach to fit whatever setting they addressed.

Lists of heroes from the Old Testament have been documented in Jewish and Christian texts, yet their common appeal to the authority of salvation history is insufficient to demonstrate a definable form. Lists were constructed for various purposes (encomiums, historical surveys, lists of exemplary people to prove certain points, and so forth), but at best they reflect a technique of appealing to sacred history that was highly adaptable to different textual settings, not the existence of a form that the author of Hebrews implemented in the writing of chapter 11.

Conclusion

To bring greater clarification to this issue, Greco-Roman, Jewish, and first-century Christian literature was searched to locate passages that not only employed lists of famous (or infamous) people, but which also sought to prove or illustrate particular points. Thus, both composition and function were used as criteria for determining the suitability of texts. To qualify for inclusion in the study, each list had to be a distinct enough entity within a document that it could be distinguished from its surrounding context, however well integrated it was.[46]

---

[46]Consequently, documents like Plutarch's *On the Bravery of Women* were excluded. Although Plutarch seeks to demonstrate the virtues of women by giving descriptions first of groups of women (243F-49F) and then of individuals (250A-63C), the magnitude of his list of brave and talented women makes calling it an example list comparable to Hebrews 11 highly questionable. It is an example book. Similarly, Philo's *Every Good Man Is Free* consists almost entirely of an extended string of examples which seeks to prove that every good person is a free person. There are subunits within the larger list, such as sections 114-30, which provide examples of noble people choosing death rather than slavery, but they are not distinctly set off from their surrounding context. This is an example discourse, and separating one set of these *exempla* from the others for analysis is problematic. Therefore, although it is possible that a rhetorical approach similar to that employed in Hebrews 11 was used in its composition, this document was excluded from consideration, in spite of the fact that Lee cites *Every Good Man Is Free* 62-130 as a *Beispielreihe* (p. 32).

The same is true for the various passages cited as parallels to Hebrews 11 from Philo's *On Rewards and Punishments:* 1ff. (Windisch and Michel), 7ff., 11 (Thyen), and 67-68

Of the different kinds of lists of famous people in the literature of antiquity, most actually do not function as examples to prove or illustrate particular points. They include, for example, (1) official or pseudo-official lists of names of contemporaries who were involved in particular events,[47] (2) genealogies, sometimes annotated to varying degrees,[48] (3) historical summaries or overviews,[49] (4) nonchronological lists of contemporaries which make no moral point,[50] (5) encomium-type lists,[51] and (6) miscellaneous other lists.[52]

In addition to these categories are the example lists of famous individuals that function to prove or illustrate particular points and whose rhetorical compositions were therefore analyzed and compared with Hebrews 11. Observing the similarities in the kinds of rhetorical techniques these example lists employ and the reasons they employ them provides valuable

---

(Lee). These passages have little in common with Hebrews 11: *On Rewards and Punishments* 1ff. deals with the three kinds of oracles written by Moses (creation of the world, history and legislation); 7ff. addresses lessons taught by Moses about rewards, honor and punishments; 11 is an example list of vocations (tradesman, ship captain, etc.); 67 is a summary and transition which concludes by saying, "We have next to consider in their turn the punishments appointed for the wicked, but in a general way since this is not the time to describe particular cases" (*Philo,* vol. VIII, trans. F. H. Colson, LCL [Cambridge: Harvard University Press, 1939] 353); and 68 initiates a description of and comments briefly upon two specific incidents: Cain's murder of Abel (68-73; cf. Gen 4:1-16) and the rebellion led by Korah (74-78; cf. Num 16:1-35). Therefore these passages from *On Rewards and Punishments* cited by Windisch, Michel, Thyen, and Lee were excluded from consideration.

[47]Ezra 2:1-70; 10:18-44; Neh 3:1-32; 7:6-73a; 10:1-27; 11:3-12:43; 1 Chron 23-27; Epistle of Aristeas 47-50; 1 Esdras 5:4-43; cf. 1 Enoch 6:7-8 and Homer, *Iliad* II.816-73.

[48]Gen 5:1-32; 10:1-32; 11:10-26; 36:1-43; 46:8-27; Matt 1:1-17; Luke 3:23-38; Pausanias, *Corinth 6.4-6, ect.*

[49]Psalm 78; Ezek 20:1-38; Judith 5:5-21; Neh 9:6-38; Sibylline Oracles III.105-61; 2 Esdras 1:4-37; 3 Macc 2:1-20; 6:1-15; Acts 7:2-53.

[50] 2 Sam 23:8-39; 1 Chron 11:10-47; T. Judah 25:1-2.

[51]Sirach 44-50; Plutarch, *On the Bravery of Women* (entire document).

[52]Such as 2 Esdras 1:38-40; Homer, *Odyssey* XI.225-332, 385-635 and page after page of annotated lists in Pausanias in which he describes the famous people of particular cities.

background information for an investigation of the rhetorical composition and function of Hebrews 11. By documenting the rhetorical techniques in Hebrews 11 and their desired effect on those who heard its words and comparing these techniques with those employed in other ancient example lists, new and valuable insights emerge for understanding the author's intention in writing Hebrews 11.

Chapter 2

Composition and Function of Example Lists

Introduction

The use of exemplary people by ancient authors to argue for or against particular viewpoints was quite common,[1] but the same cannot be said of *lists* of such examples. Lists of well-known people who function collectively as examples are relatively rare in antiquity; a broad-ranging search yielded less than thirty. Though there are certainly more such lists as yet undocumented,[2] the ones used here form a representative sample from which important observations can be made and certain conclusions drawn.

These lists are located in a wide variety of literature ranging from powerful speeches on issues of national policy by Isocrates (*To Phillip* 58-67; *Archidamus* 40-48; *Antidosis* 230-36) to Dio Chrysostom's humorous spoof, *Encomium on Hair*. They are found in a mythical tale (Homer, *Iliad* V.381-415), a rhetorical handbook (Aristotle, *Rhetoric* II.23.11); several dialogues (Cicero, *De Oratore* III.126-129, 132-136; Plutarch, *Dialogue on Love* [*Mor.*] 753D-54A, 760B-D, 760E-62A), philosophical poetry (Lucretius, *On the Nature of Things* III.1024-52), personal reflections (Marcus Aurelius, *Meditations* III.2.2-3.2; VI.47), philosophical argumentation (Plutarch, *Chance;* Philo, *On the Virtues* 198-227; 4 Maccabees

---

[1]See appendix A below for documentation from the rhetorical handbooks.

[2]Since completing my analysis of these lists, I have encountered two others: Musonius Rufus, fragment 9 in *Ioannis Stobaei: Florilegium,* vol. 2 (Lipsiae: Sumtibus et typis Caroli Tauchnitii) 70-76; and Quintilian, *Institutio Oratoria* IX.10.21-24.

18:10-19), biblical exegesis (Philo, *Who is the Heir?* 260-62), Hellenistic-Jewish Wisdom literature (Wisdom 10), sermonic exhortation (Damascus Document II.14–III.19), a last testament (1 Maccabees 2:50-64), an apocalypse (4 Ezra 7:106-111), and a pastoral letter from one church to another (1 Clement 4-6; 9:2-12:8; 17-18). No one type of literature dominates in the use of these lists. Indeed, the different styles of composition are almost as diverse as are the documents employing the lists.[3]

Judging from these twenty-five lists located in Greco-Roman, Jewish and Christian texts, there was no literary form of "example list of famous people" in antiquity. In spite of the fact that the lists have the same rhetorical function of persuading audiences, frequently the only compositional similarity between them is that they give a number of examples of famous people instead of only one or two.

The methods of presenting examples in the lists vary considerably, from extremely concise statements given in stereotyped clausal structure in which all examples are contained in one extended sentence,

> How is it that . . . Abraham prayed for the people of Sodom, and Moses for our fathers who sinned in the wilderness; and Joshua after him for Israel in the days of Achar; and Samuel in the days of Saul, and David for the plague. . . . (4 Ezra 7:106-111),[4]

to more substantial descriptions of the actions of the individuals named (Philo, *On the Virtues* 198-227). Comparing and contrasting the composition of different lists by the same individuals is even possible, since more than one example list was located in the writings of six of the ancient authors. Again, diversity is the norm. With the exception of Clement of Rome,

---

[3]See Michael R. Cosby, "The Rhetorical Composition and Function of Hebrews 11 in Light of Example-Lists in Antiquity" (Ph.D. diss., Emory University, 1985) 45-169, for a detailed analysis of each list.

[4]Trans. G. H. Box, in *The Apochrypha and Pseudepigrapha of the Old Testament in English*, vol. 2, ed. R. H. Charles (Oxford: Clarendon Press, 1913). Aristotle, *Rhet.* II.23.11 is another example of a list contained in one long sentence.

who copied the technique of Hebrews 11,[5] none of the writers appears to have implemented a form when composing a list.

From list to list there is some repetition of the use of particular rhetorical techniques, but these appear to result from the dynamics of assembling a string of examples, not reliance upon a literary or rhetorical form. In other words, the process of compiling a list tends to elicit certain rhetorical techniques, especially those that have the effect of making the examples cited appear to represent a great many other exemplary people who could also be used as evidence.

Hebrews 11 likewise uses its examples to indicate that the author has a vast number of potential examples that he could also use to prove his point. By beginning each example in 11:3-31 with πίστει, the author conveys the impression of being able to go on giving even more examples from salvation history to demonstrate the truth of what he said about faith in the introductory comments in 11:1-2. And, as will be discussed in chapter 5, when this use of anaphora ceases at 11:31, he replaces its effect with a series of other techniques in 11:32-38.

Length and Format of Example Lists

There is considerable variation in both the format and the length of examples in the lists studied. Some are very concise, giving only the names of the people and brief references to their activities, typically in a series of

---

[5]Note, e.g., the use of the concept of Jesus as High Priest in 1 Clem 36:1 followed in 36:3-5 by the same OT quotations used in Heb 1:5, 7 and 13 (Pss 104:4; 2:7-8). R. N. Grant and H. H. Graham (*The Apostolic Fathers,* vol. 2 [New York: Thomas Nelson and Sons, 1965] 104) list the following as allusions to Hebrews: 1 Clem 9–12 ◊ Heb 11 as a model; 1 Clem 13:1; 16:2 (cf. 8:1; 22:1; 45:2) ◊ Heb 3:7; 10:15 (formula); 1 Clem 17:1 ◊ Heb 11:37; 1 Clem 21:9 ◊ Heb 4:12; 1 Clem 27:2 ◊ Heb 6:18; 1 Clem 36:1 ◊ Heb 2:17; 3:1; 4:15; 1 Clem 36:2-5 ◊ Heb 1:3-5, 7, 13; 1 Clem 43:1 ◊ Heb 3:2, 5; 1 Clem 64 ◊ Heb 12:9. Clement frequently uses OT citations found in NT writings, but he never mentions any reliance upon them as secondary sources. At times it is difficult to know if he is using a NT text or merely drawing from some common fund of OT proof texts employed by Christians. In 1 Clem 49 he quotes Prov 10:12 with no citational formula, and the wording agrees with 1 Pet 4:8 and not the LXX. For a longer explanation of 1 Clement's literary dependence on Hebrews, see P. Ellingworth, "Hebrews and 1 Clement: Literary Dependence or Common Tradition," *BibZeit* 23 (1979): 262-69.

clauses composed so that each has the same or nearly the same clausal format. Such brevity is more common in the Jewish lists (see 1 Maccabees 2:50-64; 4 Maccabees 18:10-19; and 4 Ezra 7:106-11). Among Greco-Roman lists only that in Aristotle's *Rhetoric* II.23.11 is composed in this way.[6]

Other lists provide brief explanatory material about each person they mention (Homer's *Iliad* 381-415, Isocrates' *Antidosis* 230-36 and Philo's *Who is the Heir?* 260-62), and still others have examples containing detailed information about each figure in the list (Isocrates' *Archidamus* 40-48 and Philo's *On the Virtues* 198-227). Most of the lists, however, have examples varying in length, sometimes making only a passing reference to one person yet giving a lengthy description of another. For example, Cicero's *De Oratore* III.32.127-29 gives a lengthy comment on Hippias, an orator from Elis, and then merely mentions in the broadest of terms the next three men in the list:

> What shall I say about Prodicus of Ceos or Thrasymachus of Chalcedon or Protagoras of Abdera? each of whom both lectured and wrote what was considered in their period a great amount on natural science as well.[7]

A lengthy example about Gorgias of Leontini follows this comment, so the list begins and ends with a lengthy example and has three brief examples joined into one and sandwiched in the middle. On the other hand, in Isocrates' *To Phillip* 58-66 the first two examples of Alcibiades and Conon are lengthy, while the third on Dionysius is half as long and the last on Cyrus comprises only one sentence. Conversely, in Wisdom 10 the examples get progressively longer throughout the list.[8] In still other lists the length of the examples is quite random (Plutarch, *Dialogue on Love* 753D-54A, 760B-D, and 760E-62A; CD II.14-III.19; and 1 Clement 9-12).

In several lists some of the examples become quite detailed, but not because the material they contain is particularly relevant to the main point

---

[6]Plutarch's *Chance* (*Mor.* 97C-E) has very short examples but not stereotyped sentence structure. For other ways in which Greco-Roman and Jewish/Christian lists differ, see appendix B.

[7]Cicero, *De Oratore*, book III, trans. E. W. Sutton, LCL (Cambridge: Harvard University Press, 1942) 101.

[8]Cf. 1 Clem 17–18.

the author begins the list to demonstrate. In a manner quite different from the focused information about faith in Hebrews 11:1-40, a few of the authors simply become so engrossed in telling stories that they go off on tangents, providing extraneous information on particular people (for example, Plutarch, *Dialogue on Love* 761B-62A; 1 Clement 9-12 and 17-18). Variation in composition, not unity of form, is the norm when these lists are compared with each other.

Hebrews 11 joins those lists containing examples of varying lengths. Abraham and Moses receive the longest statements in verses 8-10, 17-19, and 23-28, while in verse 32 merely the names of five individual Old Testament figures and one group are listed ("time does not allow me to mention Gideon, Barak, Samson, Jephthah, David, and Samuel, and the prophets"), and in verses 33-38 the names of the people who match the descriptive statements are not provided ("those who through faith conquered kings, worked righteousness, attained promises, . . . "). In the main section of the list (3-31), with the exception of the anaphoric use of πίστει, the composition of the individual examples is almost a study in diversity. Introductory word order, length, sentence structure, and use of dependent clauses all vary considerably. There are even two sermonic explanations inserted into the text at verse 6 and verses 13-16 that are distinct from the examples.[9]

In Hebrews 11:3-31, the most diversity exists in verses 3-19, where the examples tend to deal with a wider variety of topics pertaining to faith than in verses 20-31, where the examples tend to be shorter and of similar length, with several having almost identical structures. With reduced length comes greater uniformity, and the examples take on more of a rhythmic cadence in their oral presentation. Thus, the more they approach the shorter length

---

[9]Whereas the examples in Heb 11:3-31 all begin with πίστει, the sermonic explanations at 11:6 and 13-16 have a structure that sets them apart from the examples. Verse 6 begins with χωρὶς δὲ πίστεως and applies the preceding material to his audience through a universal statement that apart from faith it is impossible to please God. Verse 13 begins with κατὰ πίστιν; and instead of giving a universal application, it introduces a commentary on the patriarchs, explaining why their actions were motivated by faith. Cf. also the reflections in 11:10, 19, and 25-26, as well as similar passages in Isocrates, *Antidosis* 233; Cicero, *De Oratore* III.128, 140; Wis 10:7-8; 1 Clem 4:7; 11:2; 12:7-8.

of the examples in texts like Aristotle, *Rhetoric* II.23.11 and 1 Maccabees 2:51-64, the more they resemble the stereotyped structures of these lists. For example, in the examples of Jacob and Joseph, the first lines of verses 21 and 22 have the sequence: "By faith" plus the name ("Jacob" or "Joseph") plus "dying" plus " . . . the sons of Joseph/Israel" plus an aortist verb.

Πίστει Ἰακὼβ ἀποθνῄσκων ἕκαστον τῶν υἱῶν Ἰωσήφ εὐλόγησεν
                    καὶ προσεκύνησεν ἐπὶ τὸ ἄκρον τῆς ῥάβδου αὐοῦ.
Πίστει Ἰωσὴφ τελευτῶν περὶ τῆς ἐξόδου τῶν υἱῶν Ἰσραὴλ ἐμνημόνευσεν
                    καὶ περὶ τῶν ὀστέων αὐτοῦ ἐνετείλατο.

By faith Jacob, when dying, each of the sons of Joseph blessed
                    and he worshipped over the top of his staff.
By faith Joseph, when dying, concerning the exodus of the sons of Israel remembered
                    and concerning his bones he commanded.

Although the second lines of these two verses differ structurally, the cadence when spoken is similar, and the resulting rhythmical quality of the two examples is quite close. The similarity of content, with both Jacob and Joseph making deathbed pronouncements, is therefore enhanced by the similarity of their composition.

Likewise, the structures of verses 27-29 resemble each other closely enough to create a noticeable repetition of cadence in an oral reading of these examples. Each begins with πίστει plus an aorist verb plus an accusative noun; and the second lines of each, although diversely formulated, are of approximately the same length. The result is that verses 27-29 have a very similar cadence when read aloud, and this resemblance strongly enhances the similarity of content. All three examples deal with the Exodus,[10] and their compositional uniformity helps to establish their common subject matter. Thus, after showing in the more discursive examples in verses 23-26 that Moses was set apart for the work of delivering the people of God, and that his choice to commit himself to God's will in-

---

[10]For explanations of why Heb 11:27 refers to the Exodus and not Moses' fearful flight to Midian, see, e.g., Westcott, 375; Montefiore, 204; and Spicq, 1:359. More will be said on this below in ch. 4.

volved rejection of worldly pleasures for the sake of heavenly reward, the Exodus is described with rhetorically balanced examples.

In none of these three examples is the subject explicitly stated. Moses is presupposed as the subject of the verbs κατέλιπεν (left behind) and πεποίηκεν (made) in verses 27-28, and in verse 29 the Israelite people are the subjects of the verb διέβησαν (passed through). The pattern of presentation in verses 27-29, however, is broken in verse 30, which is shorter and specifies its subject: "the walls of Jericho." Also, instead of the subject exercising faith to accomplish the event described, as in the previous examples, the subject in verse 30 is the inanimate wall that received the action that resulted from the faith of the Israelites. Instead of saying "by faith they encircled the wall of Jericho for seven days and it fell," which would coincide with the composition of verse 29, verse 30 reads, "by faith the walls of Jericho fell, being encircled for seven days." The shift in composition signals a shift in events, for verses 30-31 deal with the conquest of the land, not the Exodus from Egypt.

In spite of the fact that verses 30-31 both describe aspects of the destruction of Jericho, they do not reveal the same degree of similarity that the examples of the Exodus do in verses 27-29. Rahab is the subject of verse 31, and her faith inspires the action that saves her life, namely her receiving the Israelite spies. A certain degree of similarity does exist between verses 30 and 31, however, for each has the following structure: πίστει plus a nominative noun plus a verb plus a participial phrase explaining the event that occurred as a result of faith. Were it not for τοῖς ἀπειθήσασιν (the disobedient) at the end of verse 31a, the composition of the two examples would be quite parallel.

Following the main body of the list in verses 1-31 is a rhetorical transition at verse 32 that introduces the summary section (καὶ τί ἔτι λέγω, "What shall I yet say?"). There is considerable difference in the composition of the two sections of Hebrews 11. At 11:32 the anaphoric use of πίστει drops out, as does the listing of specific deeds of faith performed by the exemplary heroes of faith. Hebrews 11:32-40 is comprised primarily of sets of names and descriptive words and phrases arranged into a series of smaller groupings. The unity of each of these is enhanced by rhetorical techniques that help to tie them together, yet the composition of these groupings shows considerable diversity. The unifying characteristic is the tendency to compose each subsection in a manner that produces a staccato rhythm when delivered orally: verse 32, a series of names, gives no comment on the actions of the people it lists; verses 33-34, a series of phrases of similar length and composition, describe actions taken by famous people from salvation history without mentioning who accomplished any of the actions; verse 37, a series of words and short phrases that describe how faithful people have suffered, connects no names with its descriptions; and verse 38, a series of words and brief phrases describing how some of God's faithful who suffered for their faith had to live in exile, does not specify the names of any of those who so suffered.

In conclusion, unlike the shorter example lists with their stereotyped structures, Hebrews 11 is long enough to show considerable diversity in the composition of its component parts. Nevertheless, certain techniques are used to give uniformity to its contents. Unity of expression is attained in verses 3-31 with the anaphoric use of πίστει, as well as the structural similarities of some of the examples that form subsets within the larger structure. Unity of expression in verses 32-38, however, is established through using rhetorical techniques that produce a staccato effect in the listing of names and descriptive words and phrases. In summary, verses 1-2 introduce the topic of faith, verses 3-31 provide examples of individuals from salvation history, verses 32-38 summarize the intent of the list by emphasizing that many more examples could also be marshalled if time and space permitted, and verses 39-40 conclude and apply the example list.

The structure of the examples of famous people in Hebrews 11 varies considerably within the overall tightly knit and well-defined purpose of the list. The diversity of composition prevents a public reading of the passage from becoming monotonous, while the unity of all the examples in presenting the central theme of the chapter prevents the audience from missing the impact of the presentation. The following examination of Hebrews 11:1-40 will reveal how the author implemented rhetorical techniques to accomplish his artistic act of persuasion.

Chapter 3

Rhetorical Definition of Faith: Hebrews 11:1-2

Rhetorical Definitions and Hebrews 11:1

The debate continues over whether Hebrews 11:1 is a definition of faith, how one should translate ὑπόστασις and ἔλεγχος, and whether the introduction to the example list extends through verse 2 or verse 3. Since 11:3 speaks of the creation of the cosmos instead of an action by one of the "elders" of verse 2, some argue that the introduction to the list extends through 11:3.[1] Yet from a rhetorical perspective, the listing of examples clearly begins with the first anaphoric use of πίστει in verse 3, even though this verse does not contain a description of an "elder" that one would expect to follow verse 2.[2] The introduction consists of verses 1-2, a statement on faith connected by the use of γάρ to an assertion that because of such faith God commended the elders.[3]

---

[1]E.g., Moffatt, 158; Buchanan, 184; Bruce, 280.

[2]Vanhoye, 184-85, demonstrates from a literary perspective that 11:1-2 comprises the introduction, noting among other things that v. 39 echoes the introduction, "And all of them, being commended through their faith . . . ," and that the anaphoric series begins with v. 3.

[3]That the author views the commendation as coming from God is clear from the context. Verse 4 states that God commended Abel for his gifts; v. 5 asserts that before Enoch was translated he was commended for pleasing God; and v. 6 explains that it is impossible to please God without faith. The word repetition of μαρτυρέω and εὐαρεστέω connect vv. 1-6 into a unity of thought on this matter.

The examples that follow in verses 3-31 are rhetorically connected to verses 1-2 through the anaphoric use of πίστει, and, with varying degrees of effectiveness, they show how confidence in realities now invisible to the physical eye motivated the commendable actions of noteworthy individuals of the past. Verse 3 simply is not totally consistent with what one would expect to follow verse 2,[4] but this does not make the example ineffective. Appealing to the shared belief of the author and his audience that the world was created out of invisible elements,[5] verse 3 does not initiate the list with a πρεσβύτερος (elder) but with a statement about the beginning of the earth. In this exposition of the unchanging nature of faith, the author begins with an affirmation that the Christian's ultimate view of reality is based on a faith commitment, believing that what can be seen came from what cannot be seen.

Hebrews 11:1-2 functions both as an introduction to the example list and as a way of integrating it with the author's exhortation in 10:19-39. John Calvin recognized this connection long ago when he wrote, "Whoever made this the beginning of the eleventh chapter, has unwisely disjointed the context."[6] Of course, as Vanhoye points out, 11:1 does announce a new section as the exposition of 11:1-40 builds on the exhortation of 10:19-39 and leads into the exhortation of 12:1-13.[7] But the courageous faith encouraged in Hebrews 10 is the same valiant faith illustrated in Hebrews 11, and 11:1-2 functions both to initiate the example list and to integrate it into the larger context of the sermon.

---

[4]See Vanhoye, 184-85.

[5]Philip E. Hughes provides a lengthy explanation of why Heb 11:3 does not imply *creatio ex nihilo* in his work "The Doctrine of Creation in Hebrews 11:3," *Biblical Theology Bulletin* 2 (1972): 64-77. Similarly, Windisch, 99, says that 11:3 does not mean creation from nothing but from forms according to the heavenly archetypal images which through the Word called forth the world; and Montefiore, 188, believes v. 3 indicates creation from invisible material. For an argument for *creatio ex nihilo,* see Bruce, 281, who cites as parallels 2 Macc 7:28; 2 Baruch 21:4; and 2 Enoch 25:1ff.

[6]Calvin, 260.

[7]Vanhoye, 195-96. Cf. J. Swetnam, "Form and Content in Hebrews 7-13," *Biblica* 55 (1974): 338-48.

Although 11:1-2 efficiently performs the task for which it was created, it is certainly not as rhetorically effective as the introductions to the example lists of Isocrates in *To Philip* 57, *Archidamus* 40, *Antidosis* 230-31, or of Philo in *On the Virtues* 198. Note, for example, the powerful way in which Isocrates integrates an example list into his overall argument with the following introduction:

> That it is not, therefore, impossible for you to bring these cities together, I think has become evident to you from what I have said. But more than that, I believe I can convince you by many examples that it will also be easy for you to do this. For if it can be shown that other men in the past have undertaken enterprises which were not, indeed, more noble or more righteous than that which I have advised, but of greater magnitude and difficulty, and have actually brought them to pass, what ground will be left to my opponents to argue that you will not accomplish the easier task more quickly than other men the harder? (*To Philip* 57)[8]

The author of Hebrews was evidently not interested in producing the same kind of rhetorical effect that Isocrates desired.

When compared to other example lists, however, the introduction to Hebrews 11 is much stronger than those found, for example, in Lucretius, *On the Nature of Things* 1024 and 4 Ezra 7:106. Indeed, some lists contain no introductions at all (M. Aurelius III.2.2–3.2; Plutarch, *Dialogue on Love* 760E-62A; Wisdom 10; and 1 Clement 4-6). Also worth noting is the fact that Hebrews 11 is the only example list studied that begins with a definition of the key concept described by the list (or with any definition, for that matter).

In some ways it is unfair to compare Hebrews 11:1-2 with the rhetorical sophistication of Isocrates' introductions, for the author of Hebrews was not writing a formal speech to persuade the governing council of a city-state. His sermon is obviously of considerably different scope than the speeches delivered by famous orators in public debates. In such speeches the precise definition of a term might be of great significance, for a court case might be won or lost according to whether or not the orator's definition was able to withstand close scrutiny. Consequently, the rhetorical

---

[8]*Isocrates,* vol. 1, trans. G. Norlin, LCL (New York: G. P. Putnam's Sons, 1928) 281.

handbooks provide explanations of the rhetorical use of definitions in formal debate:

> Definition in brief and clear-cut fashion grasps the characteristic qualities of a thing, as follows: "The sovereign majesty of the republic is that which comprises the dignity and grandeur of the state." Again: "By an injury is meant doing violence to some one, to his person by assault, or to his sensibilities by insulting language, or to his reputation by some scandal." Again: "This not economy on your part, but greed, because economy is careful conservation of one's own goods, and greed is wrongful covetousness of the goods of others." . . . Definition is accounted useful for this reason: it sets forth the full meaning and character of a thing so lucidly and briefly that to express it in more words seems superfluous, and to express it in fewer is considered impossible. (*Ad Her.* IV.25.35)[9]

Quintilian is more elaborate in his discussion of the use of definition. In part he states,

> Definition is the statement of the fact called in question in appropriate, clear and concise language. . . . It consists mainly in the statement of *genus, species, difference* and *property.* For example, if you wish to define a horse . . . the *genus* is animal, the *species* mortal, the *difference* irrational (since man also is mortal) and the *property* neighing. Definition is employed by the orator for a number of different reasons. For sometimes, though there may be no doubt as to a term, there is a question as to what it includes, or, on the other hand, there may be no doubt about the thing, but no agreement as to the term to be applied to it. When the term is agreed, but the thing doubtful, conjecture may sometimes come into play, as, for instance, in the question, "What is god?" For the man who denies that god is a spirit permeating all things, assuredly asserts that the epithet "divine" is falsely applied to his nature, like Epicurus, who gives him a human form and makes him reside in the intermundane space. While both use the same term *god,* both have to employ conjecture to decide which of the two meanings is consistent with fact. (*Inst. Or.* VII.3.2-5)[10]

---

[9]*Rhetorica ad Herennium,* trans. H. Caplan, LCL (Cambridge: Harvard University Press, 1937) 317. For an analysis of this document's use of examples, see appendix A below.

[10]*The Institutio Oratoria of Quintilian,* vol. 3, trans. H. E. Butler, LCL (New York: G. P. Putnam's Sons, 1922) 49.

Quintilian goes on to explain in VII.3.6-13 that court cases can hinge on whether or not the definition of a term applies to specific cases. For example, if a man is caught in a brothel with another man's wife, is he to be considered guilty of adultery? (In other words, does adultery, the meaning of which is clear, apply to this specific instance?) Other cases might depend on which of two terms should be applied to an action. For example, to argue that an act was theft but not sacrilege, one would have to define both terms and demonstrate that the act was the one and not the other.

In the case of Hebrews 11:1, however, the author does not build his entire argument on his definition of faith. Functionally, the definition is formulated to validate the exhortation delivered in 10:19-39, and its validity is illustrated in the numerous examples that follow in 11:3-38.[11] Observing this has led various commentators to deny the status of a formal definition to 11:1. Calvin, for example, asserts that

> greatly mistaken are they who think that an exact definition of faith is given here; for the Apostle does not speak here of the whole of what faith is, but selects that part of it which was suitable to his purpose, even that it has patience connected with it.[12]

Similarly, Moffatt states that the author is not abstractly defining faith but describing it in light of the examples that follow.[13] Westcott explains that "the order (ἔστιν δὲ πίστις) shows that the object of the writer is not to give a formal definition of Faith but to bring out characteristics of Faith which bear upon his argument."[14]

---

[11]See ch. 7 below.

[12]Calvin, 260.

[13]Moffatt, 160.

[14]Westcott, 351. Similarly, Spicq comments,
> Sur l'usage de commencer une définition ou une description par ἔστιν, cf. Lc. VIII, 11: ἔστιν δε αὕτη ἡ παραβολή; 1 Tim. VI, 6; I Jo. I, 5; Platon, *Banq.* 186c: ἔστι γὰρ ἰατρική, ὡς ἐν κεφαλαίῳ εἰπεῖν, ἐπιστήμη τῶν . . . ; Plutarque, *De curiosit.* 6; Philon, *Quod Deus sit immut.* 87; *Leg. alleg.* III, 211. Ici, l'auteur pourrait répondre à une question fictive—procédé courant de la diatribé: Et qu'est-ce que la foi? ἔστιν δέ: La foi est ceci. . . . Toutefois, nous n'avons pas ice une définition proprement dite de la foi (contre S. Augustin, *Enchiridion,*

While it is correct to say that Hebrews 11:1 does not qualify as a lengthy, philosophical (or scientific) definition, the rhetorical value of this verse must not be underestimated. Although not as elaborately developed as Quintilian suggests when providing the various aspects of a definition (genus, species, . . .), 11:1 does in fact state briefly and in a clear-cut fashion the characteristic qualities of faith in a manner similar to that specified in *Rhetorica ad Herennium* IV.25.35. Furthermore, when compared to the examples of definitions given above in *Rhetorica ad Herennium* IV.25.35, Hebrews 11:1 does in fact qualify as a rhetorical definition of faith, providing a capsulized summary of what the author of Hebrews says about faith in his sermon as a whole. He could easily say that his definition ''sets forth the full meaning and character [of faith] . . . so lucidly and briefly that to express it in more words seems superfluous, and to express it in fewer is considered impossible'' (*Ad Her.* IV.25.35).[15]

Composition of Hebrews 11:1

The definition in 11:1 is formulated with two brief clauses that describe the author's understanding of faith.

ἔστιν δὲ πίστις ἐλπιζομένων ὑπόστασις,
πραγμάτων ἔλεγχος οὐ βλεπομένων.

Attempting to retain the Greek word order makes nonsense in English; so most translations produce renderings that give the two clauses of 11:1 parallel structure, thus making them synonymous in meaning.

Now faith is the substance of things hoped for,
the evidence of things not seen. (KJV)

Now faith is the assurance of things hoped for,
the conviction of things not seen. (RSV)

Now faith means we are confident of what we hope for,
convinced of what we do not see. (Moffatt)

---

i; P.L. XL,235; S. Jérome, *Ad Gal.* 5; Théodoret, Théophylacte, Delitzch, Lenski), mais une description en fonction de l'espérance et du contexte; ''describit fidem'' (S. Thomas). (Spicq, 2:336)

[15]*Rhetorica ad Herennium,* 317.

Now faith is the substance of things hoped for,
> the test of things (objects) not seen. (Westcott)

Now faith is [the] groundwork of things hoped for,
> [the] basis for testing things not seen. (Buchanan)

Now faith is being sure of what we hope for
> and certain of what we do not see. (NIV)

The parallel clausal structures of these translations reproduce some of the rhythmical quality of the original definition, but they may be somewhat deceptive. Repetition of the same word order in the second clause in English more accurately represents the construction of the antithesis of the Greek text in 10:39 than it does the Greek in 11:1.

10:39 ἡμεῖς δὲ οὐκ ἐσμὲν ὑποστολῆς εἰς ἀπώλειαν
> ἀλλὰ πίστεως εἰς περιποίησιν ψυχῆς.

11:1 ἔστιν δὲ πίστις ἐλπιζομένων ὑπόστασις,
> πραγμάτων ἔλεγχος οὐ βλεπομένων.

The repeated clausal structure of 10:39 could have been produced in 11:1 simply by saying,

> ἔστιν δὲ πίστις ὑπόστασις ἐλπιζομένων,
> ἔλεγχος οὐ βλεπομένων.

Πραγμάτων is not necessary for making clear the meaning, and such a rewording of the definition would produce a very persuasive *sounding* sentence. The resulting two statements on faith would have parallel composition of nearly equal length and cadence. Furthermore, there would be strong paronomasia between πίστις and ὑπόστασις, in addition to the sound repetition of the -ομενων genitive participial ending for both clauses. In fact, this possible reformulation would cause the Greek text to reproduce the requirement of Aristotle's specification that paromoiosis (similarity of final syllables)

> must take place at the beginning or end of the clauses. At the beginning the similarity is always shown in entire words; at the end, in the last syllables, or the inflections of one and the same word, or the repetition of the same word. (*Rhet.* III.9.9)[16]

---

[16]Aristotle, *Rhetoric*, trans. J. H. Freese, LCL (New York: G. P. Putnam's Sons, 1926) 393.

But the author of Hebrews did not compose his definition of faith in this clearly parallel manner.

If the second clause of the definition were truly parallel with the first as the English translations given above suggest, then ἔλεγχος would appear to be a synonym of ὑπόστασις and πραγμάτων οὐ βλεπομένων would be synonymous with ἐλπιζομένων. But, as also shown above, such a parallel construction in the Greek would have been quite simply produced. The author of Hebrews was obviously quite familiar with the Septuagint[17] and therefore with the parallel constructions so common in Hebrew poetry that are often transferred quite nicely into the Greek of the Septuagint. In addition, his awareness of rhetorical techniques could also have served as a basis for employing such a formulation. In rhetorical theory, parallelism, or *interpretatio,* is defined as a

> figure which does not duplicate the same word by repeating it, but replaces the word that has been used by another of the same meaning, as follows: "You have overturned the republic from its roots; you have demolished the state from its foundations ["Rem publicam radicitus evertisti, civitatem funditus deiecisti"]. . . . The hearer cannot but be impressed when the force of the first expression is renewed by the explanatory synonym. (*Ad Her.* IV.28.38)[18]

If Hebrews 11:1b were thus in parallel with 11:1a, the result would be a strong juxtaposition produced by immediately following the antithesis in 10:39 with synonymy in 11:1, moving directly from opposing statements to complementary ones. But the author of Hebrews did not employ this technique. Hebrews 11:1 is similar to 10:39 in that it contains no definite articles before the nouns[19] and consists of two brief phrases. Yet unlike 10:39, the second descriptive clause in 11:1 does not repeat the word order of the first.

---

[17]See, e.g., J. C. McCullough, "The Old Testament Quotations in Hebrews," *NTS* 26 (1980): 363-79. On 363 he gives a good listing of other works on the same subject.

[18]*Rhetorica ad Herennium,* 325.

[19]Westcott, 352, states that the inarticular πίστις indicates an abstract concept of faith, not specifically Christian faith. Michel, 373, says, "Zum griechischen Definitionsstil gehört hier außer dem vorangestellten ἔστιν das völlige Fehlen des Artikels."

Not only does 11:1b not appear to be parallel with 11:1a, but the possibility is quite good that considerations of *sound* were important in both the choice of words and syntax employed in 11:1a-b. The first clause defining faith in verse 1 begins with a plural genitive participle and the second ends with one ("ōn" sound). Furthermore, the second clause begins with a genitive plural noun, so that it also has an "ōn" sound in the last syllable of its first word. This sound repetition of "ōn" three times in the two clauses is enhanced by frequent occurrence of the "p" sound as well as paronomasia between πίστις and ὑπόστασις.

ἔστιν δὲ π<u>ίστις</u> ἐλ<u>πιζομένων</u> ὑπόστασις,
π<u>ραμάτων</u> ἔλεγχος οὐ βλε<u>πομένων</u>.

If the author had such rhetorical reasons for the selection and placement of the words in his definition of faith, this could be an important clue to solving the controversy surrounding the meaning of several key terms in the definition.

Scholars have long noted the care with which the author of Hebrews constructs his sentences, and Nigel Turner states that "An unusual word order seems often designed to arouse the readers' attention."[20] Turner goes on to say that the author's "careful straining after vocal impressiveness, by means of unconventional word-order, is not always quite successful" (12:23), and that he "cannot always maintain his apparent literary style, and even with his deliberately eccentric word order, he seems to relapse into Jewish Greek."[21]

Thus, there are ambiguities in the otherwise very high quality of the Greek in Hebrews, but this does not diminish the author's efforts at rhetorical effectiveness. Noting the author's attempts at "vocal impressiveness" and his "deliberately eccentric word order" is important when considering the construction of the very important transition made in Hebrews 11:1. The placement of ἔστιν at the beginning of the sentence instead of in its normal location is probably to emphasize the connection of

---

[20]N. Turner, *A Grammar of New Testament Greek*, vol. 4: *Style* (Edinburgh: T.&T. Clark, 1976) 107.

[21]Ibid., 109, 110.

11:1 with 10:39. This is a *purposive* modification, and there is good reason to believe that the construction of the rest of 11:1 is also governed by rhetorical considerations.

The Meaning of "Faith" in Hebrews 11:1

Determination of the meaning of ὑπόστασις and ἔλεγχος in Hebrews 11:1 is a matter of great controversy. In spite of lengthy studies tracing the use and development of the term ὑπόστασις, in particular,[22] no compelling consensus has developed concerning its precise meaning in Hebrews 11:1. Scholars remain divided over whether ὑπόστασις has an objective meaning ("substance") or a subjective meaning ("confidence"). The term occurs only five times in the New Testament—2 Corinthians 9:4; 11:17; Hebrews 1:3; 3:14; and 11:1—but the rich and varied use outside the New Testament provides fertile ground for linguistic digging.

In Hebrews 1:3 the description of Jesus as having the χαρακτήρ of God's ὑπόστασις seems to attribute to ὑπόστασις the objective meaning of "substance"; but in 3:14 ὑπόστασις appears to designate the "confidence" Christians are to maintain until the end (compare the similar meaning in 2 Corinthians 9:4; 11:17). One therefore could justify translating ὑπόστασις in Hebrews 11:1 either way on the basis of its use elsewhere in the same document. Translations giving the meaning "substance" include Beza, the Vulgate, Syriac Peshitta, KJV, ARV, NEB; and commentators supporting this view include Chrysostom, Theophylact, Theodoret, Erasmus, Calvin, Zwingli, Owen, Héring, Westcott, and Buchanan. Without exception the Greek Fathers opted for this meaning, and it continued to dominate exegesis until well into the Reformation period. Calvin, after commenting that God gives knowledge of what cannot be seen, asserts, "Faith . . . is . . . the . . . substance [*substantia*] of things which are as yet the objects of hope and the evidence of things not seen."[23]

In order to conform to contemporary research on the meaning of faith in Hebrews as a whole, more recent commentators who maintain this view

---

[22]See, e.g., the bibliography in Koester, ὑπόστασις in *TDNT* 8:572; plus the lengthy investigations by Bleek, 721-27, and Spicq, 2:336-38.

[23]Calvin, 262.

Reserv

Rhetorical Comp
+ function

Crosby, Michael

BS 2775.2.
C 67 1988

of "substance" have modified the earlier formulations of the Greek Fathers and those who followed their thinking. Westcott argues that ἔλεγχος is the proof or test of the reality of the unseen, and ὑπόστασις is " 'that which gives true existence' to an object."[24] "For it is in the virtue of faith that things hoped for *are* now, so that faith is their essence in regard to the actual experience of the believer."[25] Helmut Koester states that "in Hb. ὑπόστασις always denotes the 'reality' of God which stands contrasted with the corruptible, shadowy, and merely prototypical character of the world but which is paradoxically present in Jesus and is the possession of the community as faith."[26]

> Primarily, then, ἔλεγχος and ὑπόστασις do not describe faith but define the character of the transcendent future things, and do so in the same sense as Philo and other representatives of Middle Platonism speak of the reality and actuality of God and the world of ideas. In a formulation of incomparable boldness Hb. 11:1 identifies πίστις with this transcendent reality: Faith is the reality of what is hoped for in exactly the sense in which Jesus is called the χαρακτήρ of the reality of the transcendent God in 1:3. The one formulation is as paradoxical as the other to the degree that the presence of the divine reality is found in the one case in the obedience of a suffering and dying man (cf. Hb. 5:7) and in the other in the faith of the community. But this is the point of Hb. Only the work of this Jesus and only participation in this work (= faith) are not subject to the corruptibility of the merely shadowy and prototypical.[27]

So strongly does Koester believe his linguistic study to be correct that he labels the very common interpretation of ὑπόστασις as "confidence" to be "untenable."[28]

The initial published interpretation of ὑπόστασις as "confidence" apparently occurred when Melanchthon convinced Luther to employ the meaning "sure confidence," thus introducing the element of personal

---

[24]Westcott, 352.

[25]Ibid., 353.

[26]Koester, ὑπόστασις, *TDNT* 8: 587-88.

[27]Ibid., 587

[28]Ibid., 586.

conviction in the definition of faith in 11:1.[29] Since Luther's time this new element of personal conviction has been dominant in Protestant exegesis.[30] Examples of scholars who take this meaning include Tyndale, Menegoz, Baur, Moffatt, Windisch, Scott, Bruce, and Montefiore, and it is reflected in such recent translations as the RSV, NIV, and NASV. Moffatt, for example, argues that the Greek Fathers' belief that Hebrews 11:1 gives an abstract definition of faith misled them to view ὑπόστασις as "substance."[31] According to Moffatt, faith does not impart reality to creation (verse 3) or any real existence to unseen things. Faith is believing with absolute confidence in the unseen things of God, and the best definition of it is found in verse 27: "seeing Him who is invisible."[32] Thus, faith is approximately equivalent to Paul's ἐλπίς. Hebrews 11:1 is not an abstract definition but a description of faith in light of what follows: "an active conviction which moves and molds human conduct."[33] Similarly, Büchsel asserts,

> A faith which of itself contained or offered proof of things unseen would not be the faith of Hb., which stands on the revelation, Word and promise of God and has nothing but what it receives. Thus faith is confidence in what is hoped for, since it is the divinely given conviction of things unseen.[34]

Among the other explanations in the secondary literature,[35] Gerhard Dautzenberg's "Der Glaube im Hebräerbrief" is valuable.[36] He observes that πίστις and ἐλπίς are largely interchangeable in Hebrews, being used alternately on stylistic grounds (for example, 6:11-12; compare 3:6,

---

[29]H. Dorrie, "ὑπόστασις. Wört-und Bedeutungsgeschichte," *NGG philologisch-hist. Klasse* (1955) 3, 35-92.

[30]See Koester, *TDNT* 8: 586.

[31]Moffatt, 160.

[32]Ibid., 161.

[33]Ibid., 160.

[34]Büchsel, ἔλεγχος in *TDNT* 2: 476.

[35]Spicq, 2: 336-40, gives a very detailed review of the options for this verse.

[36]*BibZeit* 17 (1973): 161-77.

14). Admittedly, "hope" is generally not used in Hebrews, but "faith" is normally engraved with the meaning of "hope," as 11:13 clearly demonstrates (compare verses 9, 10, 24-26, 39).[37] Since unbelief and disobedience are opposites of belief in the promise (3:12, 18-19), faithful and obedient acceptance of the Christian message is necessary for obtaining the promise.[38]

Dautzenberg notes that faith in Hebrews does not, as in Paul, designate a belief that God raised Jesus Christ from the dead, but it indicates an attitude of patient endurance best illustrated by Jesus' own bearing of the cross (10:36; 12:1-2; compare 5:7).[39] Thus, he concludes that the focus of faith in Hebrews is upon steadfastness and truth and is based on invisible things. To say that ὑπόστασις in 11:1 means "reality" or "substance" would be to affirm a paradoxical notion that faith is the reality of things hoped for, whereas the meaning "steadfastness" (or "determination") clearly gives faith the element of personal attitude that so characterizes it in the preceding material. Dautzenberg also points out that since the author's literary style is to connect passages to the material preceding them, it is consistent that he should juxtapose faithfulness and apostasy in 11:1 as he did in the exhortation of chapter 10.

Unlike many scholars, Dautzenberg does not believe that ὑπόστασις and ἔλεγχος are synonymous in 11:1. Relying upon linguistic studies by Büchsel and Baur, he states that ἔλεγχος cannot have a subjective meaning,[40] so he concludes that it must designate the noetic aspect of faith which precedes the exalted witness of faith in 11:3ff. Thus, while Dautzenberg argues that the meaning of ἔλεγχος outside of Hebrews is determinative for its use in 11:1, he believes that the context in Hebrews determines the otherwise ambiguous meaning of ὑπόστασις.

---

[37]Ibid., 163-64.

[38]Ibid., 165.

[39]Ibid., 167-68.

[40]Büchsel, ἔλεγχος, *TDNT* 2: 473; Baur 494; contra Grässer, *Der Glaube im Hebräerbrief* (Marburg: N. G. Elwert, 1965) 51, 528; and Windisch, 99.

This approach rejects what Büchsel calls "the necessary parallelism of ὑπόστασις and ἔλεγχος";[41] as well as H.-G. Link's opinion that the meaning of ἔλεγχος

> can be deduced only from its context in the definition of faith given in this chapter. The sentence falls into two parts. The second half is a parallelism, to be compared with the first part: *elenchos* strengthens *hypostasis,* and *pragmata ou blepomena,* things not seen, explains *elpizomena,* things hoped for. The concepts are unmistakably Hellenistic in character . . . *elenchos* should be interpreted . . . in its context in the theology of Heb. in a strictly theological sense, as referring to conviction, about the power of the future world promised by God which is here described in the language of secular Gk. as "things not seen." Heb. 11:1 would then mean: "But faith is the pledge of things hoped for, the conviction of things we cannot see."[42]

Otto Michel holds a view similar to Link's,[43] but B. F. Westcott reverses the approach. He says on the basis of external linguistic evidence that ἔλεγχος means "proof" or "test," and therefore an equivalent meaning must be given to ὑπόστασις.[44]Clearly, in addition to semantic investigations of these words, deciding whether or not 11:1b is parallel to 11:1a is extremely important in determining the meanings of ὑπόστασις and ἔλεγχος.

The rhetorical investigation conducted above adds credibility to Dautzenberg's argument against viewing 11:1 as a parallel construction. He says that the definition of faith stresses both the persisting faithfulness of God's people and their object of faith, which is the presently unseen reality of things that are hoped for. Consequently, Noah is a good example of faith, for he built the ark on the basis of godly wisdom when there was no perceivable danger to validate the oracle he had received. Likewise the patriarchs, who, although they all died without receiving the promise, saw and greeted it from afar (11:13). And concerning Moses, the author of He-

---

[41]*TDNT* 2: 476.

[42]Link, ἔλεγχω in *NIDNTTh* 2:142.

[43]Michel, 376-79.

[44]Westcott, 352.

brews says, "By faith he left Egypt, not fearing the wrath of the king, for he endured as one who sees the invisible" (11:27).[45]

The fact that Hebrews 10 clearly describes faith as stalwartly and boldly maintaining one's confidence in the truth of the Christian proclamation of heavenly hope must be taken seriously in the interpretation of 11:1. The connection between 11:1 and 10:39 is too clear to do otherwise. Also, it is doubtful that elsewhere in Hebrews faith ever gives substance to unseen realities. As the heavenly temple existed prior to the earthly copy (8:1-6; 9:11-14, 23), the new Jerusalem, the heavenly city of God which is the object of Christian hope, already exists but simply cannot be seen with physical eyes (11:10, 16; 12:22-23; 13:14).

This heavenly city is probably synonymous with the rest into which God entered on the seventh day of creation and which he promises to his faithful people (4:1-11).[46] The rebellious Israelites did not enter God's rest because they did not combine faith with their hearing of the word that was proclaimed to them (ἀλλ᾽ οὐκ ὠφέλησεν ὁ λόγος τῆς ἀκοῆς ἐκείνους μὴ συγκεκερασμένους τῇ πίστει τοῖς ἀκούσασιν, 4:2). The author makes it clear that only those who have faith actually enter this rest that has been finished since the foundations of the earth were laid (εἰσερχόμεθα γὰρ εἰς τὴν κατάπαυσιν οἱ πιστεύσαντες . . . καίτοι τῶν ἔργων ἀπὸ καταβολῆς κόσμου γενηθέντων, 4:3).

Thus, when the author urges his listeners to remain faithful to the Christian hope in 10:19-39, he tells them to come with full assurance of faith (πληροφορίᾳ πίστεως, 10:22), holding firm their confession of hope κατέχωμεν τὴν ὁμολογίαν τῆς ἐλπίδος, 10:23) and inheriting their great reward, the promise of God to those who have faith for the salvation of their souls (10:35-39). To fail to hold fast their confession because of timidity would be to experience the terrible, fiery, destructive judgment of God (10:26-31, 39). This is parallel to the warning given in 6:4-8, after which the author says in 6:9 that he believes his listeners have

---

[45]Dautzenberg, "Der Glaube," 169-70.

[46]For a major study on the concept of "Rest" in Hebrews, see O. Hofius, *Katapausis: Die Vorstellung vom endzeitlichen Ruheort im Hebräerbrief* (Tübingen: J. C. B. Mohr, 1970).

better things accompanying salvation. His desire is for them to have full assurance of hope until the end (τὴν πληροφορίαν τῆς ἐλπίδος ἄχρι τέλους, 6:11), which is another way of saying, "be imitators of those who through faith and patience inherit the promises" (μιμηταὶ δὲ τῶν διὰ πίστεως καὶ μακροθυμίας κληρονομούντων τὰς ἐπαγγελίας, 6:12). Faith is synonymous with tenaciously holding on to the heavenly hope promised by God, and in this context the author gives his definition in 11:1, integrating this introduction to the list both with the examples that follow and with the exhortation that precedes.

In conclusion, although the meanings of ὑπόστασις and ἔλεγχος in 11:1 are still disputed on purely linguistic and contextual grounds, the rhetorical dimensions of the verse shed new light on the construction of this definition of faith. The paronomasia between πίστις and ὑπόστασις, repetition of the ομενων participial endings and the ων genitive noun ending, plus repetition of the "p" sound indicate that the author paid careful attention to the way the definition *sounds*. Furthermore, the fact that he could easily have constructed 11:1 in a clearly parallel manner, which also would have had significant paronomasia, but chose instead to write phrases that are quite similar but not parallel, seems to indicate that he was attempting not to produce synonymy but a form of amplification.

By immediately following the antithesis concerning faith in 10:39 (which concludes the exhortation of 10:19-38 and draws its meaning of faith from this exhortation) with a definition of faith that is clearly connected to 10:39 by the repetition of πίστις, the author gives the essence of the kind of faith he desires his listeners to have: faith is firm confidence in the things they hope for as well as the proof of the things they cannot see. The heavenly reward for which the faithful men and women of the past lived and died (11:6, 10, 13-16, 26) is the same reward the author holds before his audience (10:35, 39). Faith is not only a firm belief in the existence of this reward, but the existence of faith, leading people to turn away from worldly pleasure and security, is also proof of the existence of the heavenly reward.

Chapter 4

Anaphora in Hebrews 11:3-31

Introduction

The dominant rhetorical technique in Hebrews 11, the one that is so obvious that no responsible commentator fails to mention it, is the anaphoric use of πίστει in 11:3-31 to begin each example. In spite of such attention given to this rhetorical technique, however, extremely little is said about *why* the author implements it. This is yet another indication that commentators have largely failed to recognize the importance of rhetorical technique in Hebrews as a vital part of the author's effort to persuade his audience.

Πίστει is used anaphorically eighteen times in 11:3-31, continually reinforcing the connection between the introductory statements in 11:1-2 and the specific examples of faith in the lives of famous men and women of the past. This connection is hammered into the mind of the listener by the tremendous emphasis that each notable action recorded in the list was accomplished *by faith*. Repeatedly the listener is struck by hearing πίστει and yet another example of how faith motivated the life of a worthy person of the past.

Compared to many of the other ancient example lists, Hebrews 11 strings together a relatively large number of examples, and their number is made to appear even larger by beginning each anaphorically. The mere fact that so many examples are compiled from the Scriptures strengthens the author's case that his definition of faith in 11:1 is well founded in salvation history, but the implementation of anaphora adds to the forcefulness of his message. Beginning each example with "by faith" creates a kind of rhythm of expression that gives the impression that together they represent a great many more examples that could also be cited if time and space permitted. The rhythm creates the feeling that the list could go on indefinitely because the definition of faith in 11:1 truly represents a universal statement of timeless truth. What is true for the author and his audience was true back to the time of Cain and Abel. This rhetorical impression is later given explicit expression in 11:32, where the author states that he simply does not have sufficient time to go on giving examples, although he has many more available.

Among the other example lists that employ anaphora, none approaches the extensive use of this rhetorical technique in Hebrews 11. The eighteen uses of πίστει in Hebrews 11:3-31 to initiate examples dealing with fourteen different people is in a class by itself. Among the people described, the figures of Abraham and Moses assume dominant importance. While most of the other people have one brief statement about their faith that is introduced with one use of πίστει, Abraham and Moses have multiple acts of faith recorded.[1] Πίστει is used either three or four times with reference to Abraham (verses 8, 9, 11?, 17)[2] and four times for the career of Moses (verses 23, 24, 27, 28).

---

[1]Michel, 390-91, points out this detail of structure and uses it to postulate the *Vorlage* of the text.

[2]There is some question over whether Sarah would be put forward as a hero of faith in 11:11a when the Genesis account says she laughed scornfully in response to hearing that she was going to bear a son. Textual witnesses reveal a variety of different readings: καὶ αὐτὴ Σάρρα στεῖρα, the reading favored by the Nestle-Aland 26th edition, occurs in 𝔭[46], D*, ψ, Old Latin and the Vulgate; καὶ αὐτὴ Σάρρα occurs in 𝔭[13vid·] ℵ, A, D[2], m and Augustine; καὶ αὐτὴ Σάρρα ἡ στεῖρα occurs in D[1] 6, 81, etc.; and καὶ αὐτὴ Σάρρα στεῖρα οὖσα occurs in P, 104, 365, etc. Matters are further complicated by lexical details. F. F. Bruce states that the expression εἰς καταβολὴν σπέρματος in Heb 11:11 "refers to the father's part in the generative process, not the mother's," and "the expression 'for the conception of seed' would be εἰς σύλληψιν σπέρματος" (301, n. 99). Similarly, O. Michel explains,

Ist καταβολὴ σπέρματος ein Ausdruck, der nur für den Mann paßt? Die Geschichte der Exegese ist reich an Erklärungsversuchen. καὶ αὐτή soll die Weiblichkeit ("'sie, die nur ein Weib war" Chrysostomus) oder den Unglauben der Sara ("'sie, die zuvor ungläubig gewesen war" Fr. Bleek) hervorheben. Die patristischen Ausleger verstehen καταβολή als ὑποδοχή (= Empfängnis). Der hellenistische Sprachgebrauch bezeugt καταβολή bzw. καταβάλειν als geschlechtliche Funktion des Mannes (= Befruchtung), ὑποδόχη bzw. ὑποδέχεσθαι als die der Frau. Bauer s.v. καταβολή rechnet mit der Möglichkleit, καταβολή im allgemeinen Sinn verstehen zu können ("'sie empfing die Kraft, die Nachkommenschaft zu begründen"). Ausschlaggebend ist aber die feste hellenistische Ausdrucksweise, durch die ja gerade der Anstoß am Text entsteht. (395-96; see n. 2 for a listing of the uses of καταβολή in antiquity.)

In his textual commentary, Bruce M. Metzger admits that "in Greek the expression δύναμιν εἰς καταβολὴν σπέρματος ἔλαβεν is regularly used of the male in begetting, not the female in conceiving"; so he says,

Appreciating the lexical difficulty, but unwilling to emend the text, a majority of the Committee understood the words καὶ αὐτὴ Σάρρα στεῖρα to be a Hebraic circumstantial clause, thus allowing Ἀβραάμ (ver. 8) to serve as subject of ἔλαβεν ("by faith, even though Sarah was barren, he [Abraham] received power to beget . . . "). (A Textual Commentary on the Greek New Testament [London/New York: United Bible Societies, 1971] 672.)

This interpretation retains the focus of faith on Abraham in Heb 11:11-12 and brings a greater degree of unity to 11:8-19. (For a thorough survey of the various theories advanced by scholars on Heb 11:11, see Spicq, 2: 348-49.)

If Sarah is not the example of faith in v. 11, this would be one of two instances in the list where the name of a person first to be given after the initial πίστει is not overtly the object of the example. The other is in v. 23 where "Moses" comes immediately after "By faith"; but in this instance the implication seems to be that when his parents saw how beautiful Moses was, his appearance inspired faith in them.

Scholars do not appear to have considered the possible rhetorical reasons for using the phrase Σάρρα στεῖρα. This is an instance of paronomasia whose English equivalent would be something like "Sterile Cheryl." It heightens the impact of the miraculous nature of offspring coming from an elderly couple past the years of childbearing and forms a trilogy with two following statements detailing the physical impossibility of the event: Sterile Sarah received power to conceive (or Abraham received power to conceive seed even in sterile Sarah; or together with Sarah, Abraham received power to conceive) (11a) . . . beyond the age of childbearing (11b) . . . from one who was dead (12b). The unity of this section is rhetorically established through the use of καί in either the first or second position in five of the six clauses in vv. 11-12 (καθώς is used in 12c). Verses 8-10 form a unit: note the omission of Abraham's name in 11:9 and the use of aorist verbs at the beginning of these examples which differs from the preceding examples. This pattern is broken in v. 11.

One reason the section dealing with Abraham[3] occupies such a large portion of the list (verses 8-19) is the presence of the homiletical insertion of verses 13-16. It is interesting that this brief commentary reflects upon the content of 11:8-10, not the material in 11:11-12 which immediately precedes it. Hebrews 11:13-16 actually separates the two examples dealing with the miraculous birth and preservation of Isaac (verses 11-12 and 17-19), making the little homily seem somewhat out of place.

The first Abraham example in verse 8 speaks of his obedient exit from Mesopotamia, and the second in verse 9 focuses on his dwelling in the land of promise as a sojourner. Connected to verse 9 by the use of γάρ is a mini-commentary (verse 10) which explains why Abraham could continue to view himself as a sojourner in the land God had promised to him. Following this homiletical reflection on verse 9 is another example comprised of verses 11-12 that changes the focus from the promised land to the promised heir and the establishment of the chosen people, emphasizing the miraculous nature of the birth of Isaac from parents past the age of childbearing. The most lengthy homiletical comment in Hebrews 11 follows in verses 13-16, but it does not reflect upon Isaac's miraculous birth. It explains the significance of the preceding examples by asserting that the patriarchs all died without receiving God's promise of the land. Beginning with κατὰ πίστιν instead of πίστει as do all of the examples, this commentary expands the thought of verses 9-10. The author asserts that the patriarchs believed they would find the true fulfillment of God's promise of the land in a heavenly homeland (11:13-16), not on earth. This comment, while exhibiting close affinity to the content of verses 8-10, which speak of dwelling as sojourners on earth, has little connection with the examples immediately preceding it, 11:11-12.

By comparison, the mini commentary in verse 6 is clearly connected to the preceding example in verse 5 through repetition of εὐαρεσ-

---

[3]Westcott, 359, says that this material illuminates three different aspects of Abraham's faith: self-surrender (v. 8); patience (vv. 9-10); and influence on Sarah (vv. 11-12). Moffatt, 169-70, 176-77, also speaks of three phases of Abraham's faith: obedience (v. 8); patience (vv. 9-10); and the supreme test of faith (vv. 17-19).

τέω,[4]and by subject matter to verses 3-4. Verse 6 provides a distinct application of the examples that precede it, relating strongly to the belief in unseen realities that these verses illustrate. On the other hand, the reflection in verses 13-16 relates only to part of the preceding examples in verses 7-12. One might also notice that after verse 6 there is no more mention of the men in the preceding examples (Abel and Enoch), whereas after verses 13-16 the men mentioned in verses 7-12 (Abraham, Isaac and Jacob) are again used as examples in verses 17-21. The initial example in verses 17-19 focuses upon the miraculous preservation of the lineage of the promised heir, Isaac, when Abraham obediently set about to sacrifice him. This section has strong connections with verses 11-12, which speak of Isaac's miraculous birth and the proliferation of the chosen people.[5] The focus of the examples immediately before and after the short homiletical comment in verses 13-16, therefore, is not upon the theme of this comment. Indeed, if verses 13-16 were placed after verse 10, the connection between the explanation and its context would be stronger, and the unity of content in verses 11-12 and 17-19 would be clearer. Although one might legitimately consider 11:13-16 to be a deliberate interruption of the πίστει series so as to avoid diminishing the effect of the anaphora by satiating the audience, its exact placement in the example list seems to diminish slightly the rhetorical effectiveness.

Following the example of Abraham in 11:17-19, examples of Isaac, Jacob, and Joseph follow in rapid succession in 11:20-22.[6] With the ad-

---

[4]Michel, 386-87, says that both sayings in v. 6 serve to explain v. 5; v. 6 is a resumption of the definition of 11:1—God's existence belongs to the invisibility of heavenly things, whereas his reward is part of the Christian hope.

[5]Michel, 401, notes the close connection between 11:12 and 17, and uses this observation to comment of the *Vorlage,* saying that 11:13-16 is clearly an editorial insertion. Buchanan, 195, calls 11:17 a poetic couplet that echoes 11:11-12. Spicq, 2:355, in explaining the significance of ἐν παραβολῇ in v. 19, uses Aristotle's distinction between the two species of examples in *Rhet.* II.20.1393a: (1) citation of former deeds; (2) invention of an example, either by parable or fable. Spicq says the "parable" in 11:19 is a teaching by figurative action (cf. 11:9), like the serpent in the desert in Wis 16:6-7. Cf. the lengthy comment on ἐν παραβολῇ in Westcott, 369, and Michel, 402-403.

vent of Moses in the list, however, the pattern of one example per person is again broken. Πίστει initiates four examples of Moses in verses 23-28.[7] Although verse 23 actually describes the brave action of his parents, πίστει is connected to Moses in such a way as to indicate that it was his beauty that inspired their boldness: "By faith Moses, when born, was hidden (for) three months by his parents because they saw the beauty of the child; and they did not fear the edict of the king."[8] Verse 24 repeats the opening format of verse 23 πίστει Μωϋσης . . .), only now it is to designate the fact that Moses had grown to be a man: "By faith Moses, when he had become great, refused to be called the son of the daughter of Pharaoh."[9] As 11:10 comments upon 11:9, so verses 25-26 comment on verse 24, ascribing Christological motivations to Moses' actions: "choosing rather to suffer with the people of God than to have the temporary pleasure of sin, considering the reproach of Christ to be of greater wealth than the treasures of Egypt."

Once this theological reflection is completed, however, the next two examples of Moses' career are very brief, and there is no homiletical expansion as in verses 6 and 13-16 that is separated from the anaphorically initiated examples. Whereas 11:6 begins with χωρὶς δὲ πίστεως and verse 13 with κατὰ πίστιν, making these comments distinct from the

---

[6]Spicq, 2:356, notes this rapid succession. Michel, 403-404, notes that 11:20-22 are proportionally short and all three concern death sayings. Vanhoye, 188, states, "La suite présente une alternance rapide de bénédictions et de morts, phases positives et négatives de la marche vers la promesse."

[7]For special works on the role of Moses in Hebrews, see Mary Rose D'Angelo, *Moses in the Letter to the Hebrews,* SBL Dissertation Series 42 (Missoula MT: Scholars Press, 1979); and P. R. Jones, "The Figure of Moses as a Heuristic Device for Understanding the Pastoral Intent of Hebrews," *RevExp* 76 (1979): 95-107.

[8]Spicq, 2: 356-57, explains that Moses' parents saw his divine vocation in the grace and charm (ἀστεῖος) of their son, and therefore a spirit of faith in providence motivated them to hide him. Spicq provides a number of extrabiblical references to Moses' childhood that are helpful in interpreting Heb 11:23. See also, e.g., Westcott, 373, and Moffatt, 179, for explanations of how 11:23 indicates that Moses called forth faith in his parents.

[9]Owen, 7: 142-48, provides an extensive commentary explaining why μέγας γενόμενος in Heb 11:24 means "grown up" and not "great in government."

examples which all begin with πίστει, 11:25-26 receives no such delineation. Thus, although there are four uses of πίστει in both the section dealing with Moses and that which treats Abraham, the author of Hebrews made no attempt to make the other dimensions of these two sections conform to each other.

There is a good deal of unity among the three examples involving Moses' actions of faith: (1) identification with God's people, which meant rejection of worldly pleasure and resulted in persecution because he looked forward to his future (heavenly) reward (verses 24-26); (2) leaving Egypt in defiance of the king because he saw that which is invisible to physical eyes (verse 27); and (3) celebration of the Passover out of obedience to the unseen God (verse 28). The focus of all of the examples concerning Moses is upon his separation from the worldly environment of Egypt, and verses 27-28 deal specifically with the Exodus.[10] This exodus theme is continued in verse 29 with reference to the crossing of the Red Sea, although here the Israelite people are joined to Moses, and as a group they form the new subject. As verses 27-28 merely understand Moses as their subject, so verse 29 assumes the Israelites as its subject without specifying them by name.[11] This breaks the pattern of specifying the name of the person each time a new example is introduced with πίστει. The author of Hebrews here

----

[10]Primarily on the basis of chronological suppositions, some scholars argue that, since v. 28 describes the Exodus, v. 27 must refer to Moses' flight to Midian (e.g., Moffatt, 181-82, Bruce, 321-22). The lack of distinct chronological ordering in the examples of Abraham observed above, however, argues against such a viewpoint. Although the examples in 11:3-31 are chronologically arranged, in the cases of Abraham and Moses they are partially grouped according to topic. The very similar composition of the three examples in 11:27-29 is a telling sign that they all speak of the same event. (See comments on "format" above in ch. 2. Also see Spicq, 2:359, for an argument that both the mention of Moses' fear in Exod 2:15 and linguistic evidence on καταλείπω verify that Heb 11:27 refers to the Exodus.)

[11]This defies the normal pattern of giving the name of the hero each time a new example is introduced with πίστει, a pattern broken previously only with the second example of Abraham in v. 9 (and perhaps v. 11). Moffatt, 183, states that v. 29 is a direct sequel to v. 28, only now Moses is included with the people (cf. 3:16). Similarly, Bruce, 324, argues that all Israel is associated with Moses in this act of faith, and Westcott, 376, states that Moses imparted his faith to Israel.

merely takes for granted that his audience understands the identity of the new subject in verse 29 when he changes to a plural verb form.

The last two examples in the list, verses 30-31, skip over the Wilderness Sojourn and focus on the beginning of the conquest of the land, the destruction of Jericho. They are distinct from the previous verses describing Moses and the Israelites with respect to content as well as formulation: Whereas verses 27-29 repeat the pattern of πίστει plus an aorist verb plus an accusative noun . . . plus an explanatory clause beginning with the words γάρ, ἵνα, ἧς, verses 30-31 have the pattern πίστει plus a nominative noun plus an aorist verb . . . plus an explanatory clause beginning with a participle. Nevertheless, there is a sort of rhythmical pattern of expression in verses 27-31 that does tie these examples together. Once the Christological explanation of verses 25-26 is completed, the remaining examples are all short and progress rapidly toward the conclusion of the listing of specific individuals.[12] The momentum of their recitation is abruptly terminated with verse 32.

In conclusion, there is basically a twofold rhetorical thrust in the anaphoric use of πίστει in Hebrews 11. First, it is designed to place continually before the listener the assertion that faith was the motivation for the great deeds performed by loyal individuals of the past who received God's commendation. Second, anaphora is used to make the relatively large number of examples listed appear representative of a vast number of other examples that could also be cited. Anaphora in Hebrews 11 reveals both power in its rhetorical effect and diversity in its implementation. While for most of the famous people in the list πίστει is used once to introduce one example from that person's life, for Abraham and Moses multiple examples are given, each beginning with πίστει.

Anaphora in Other Ancient Example Lists

Since the rhetorical function of the example lists is to make their authors' viewpoints more convincing by the multiplication of evidence, it is not surprising that the dominant rhetorical techniques they employ are those that enhance the impression that only a few examples from a great pool of

---

[12]Vanhoye, 190, notes that 11:27-31 resumes the rapid rhythm of 11:20-22.

possibilities have been selected for use. Occasionally, however, an author explicitly claims to have many other possible examples that also prove his point. For example, when Isocrates seeks to bring about a pan-hellenic state by convincing Philip, king of Macedon, forcibly to bring all of the Greek city-states into a single, powerful entity which could defeat the invading Persians, he says in *To Philip* 65: "Again, there is the case of Dionysius (for I desire you to be convinced by many instances that the course of action to which I am urging you is an easy one)."[13] In *Archidamus* 47, where Isocrates tries to stir the Spartans to war with the Thebans when they were tempted instead to give up the city of Messene which the Thebans were occupying, his claim is even more explicit. After providing examples of how weaker armies had conquered stronger armies, he says, "But we should both grow weary, you with listening and I with speaking, if we were to examine every incident of this sort."[14] Typically, however, instead of making overt claims to have many other examples available, the lists employ rhetorical devices which *imply* that there are many more examples of the truth of what they seek to establish. This is done in a variety of ways, not least of which is anaphora.

Not surprisingly, 1 Clement 4-6, which imitates the pattern of Hebrews 11 in its construction, uses ζῆλος and διὰ ζῆλος anaphorically in a series of examples designed to emphasize that jealousy has *always* been a cause of great harm for godly people.[15] Similarly, in Homer's *Iliad* V.383-84, Dione subtly indicates in her example list that she has many more examples available when she seeks to comfort her bleeding daughter Aphrodite, who was wounded by Diomedes during a battle. Dione consoles Aphrodite by demonstrating that *many* other immortals had suffered at the hands of mortals, and she begins each of her three examples with τλῆ μέν (δ') (*Iliad* V.385, 392, and 395). This repetition shows continuity between the examples and reinforces Dione's introductory comment that such suffering has come upon *many* of the immortals: "for full many of us that have dwellings on Olympus have suffered (τλῆμεν) at the hands

---

[13]*Isocrates*, vol. 1, trans. G. Norlin, LCL (New York: G. P. Putnam's Sons, 1928) 285.

[14]Ibid., 373.

[15]See also the use of διὰ πίστιν καὶ φιλοξενίαν in 1 Clem 11:1a and 12:1a.

of men, in bringing grievous woes one upon the other'' (V.383-84).[16] In addition to anaphora, the structure of each of her examples is quite similar, and this combination provides a rhetorical linking of the three examples,[17] enhancing the unity of those portrayed as suffering and establishing the truth of Dione's initial claim in V.383-84: "many of us . . . have suffered. . . . So suffered Ares. . . . So suffered Hera. . . . So suffered Hades. . . ."

---

[16]Homer, *Iliad*, trans. A. T. Murray, LCL (New York: G. P. Putnam's Sons, 1924) 223.

[17]M. M. Willcock says, "Dione's speech is a good example of the use of mythological examples as a method of consolation. The three separate examples have a cumulative effect" (*A Commentary on Homer's Iliad: Books I-VI* [London: Macmillan, 1970] 170). This cumulative effect is elucidated by Dieter Lohmann, who makes the following structural observations on the list in the context of explaining compositional characteristics in the *Iliad*.

Katalogartige Aufzählungen, oft anaphorische aneinandergereiht, sind ein Mittel deskriptiver Schilderung. Die Beobachtung dass sie häufig im Zentrum einer Ringkomposition anzutreffen sind, bestätigt daher unsere bisherigen Ergebnisse. Am auffallendsten ist der Exempla-Katalog der Rede Diones 5. 382ff: Den Ring bilden die Disticha 383/4 und 403/4:

a. 383/4 In grosser Zahl litten wir, die wir *die olympischen Häuser bewohnen,* von Seiten der Menschen. . . .

Zentrum: 385-397 Drei Exempla (398-402 zu athetieren, s.u.!).

a'. 403/4 (Herakles) . . . der Frevler, der mit seinem Bogen die Götter bedrängte, die *den Olymp bewohnen.*

Die drei Exempla (7 + 3 + 3 Verse) sind steretyp eingeleitet und jeweils in gleicher Weise strukturiert:

1. Es *litt* Ares 385[a] (Hera 392[a], Hades 395).

2. Schilderung des Vorganges, jedesmal in einem temporalen Nebensatz 385[b], 392[b], 396.

3. Abschliessend des *Leiden* selbst: 391[b] . . . die harte Fessel bezwang ihn; 394[b] . . . da ergriff sie unheilbarer Schmerz; 397 (als Herakles ihn) . . . den Schmerzen auslieferte.

(Also jeweils ein RK im Kleinen: 1. Leiden allgemein—3. Leiden speziell) Jedes Paradeigma ist somit in gleicher Weise gegliedert, die Verse 398-402 sind daher deutlich als späterer Zusatz erkennbar. (*Die Komposition der Reden in der Ilias,* Untersuchungen zun antiken Literatur und Geschichte, Band 6 [Berlin: Walter de Gruyter & Co., 1970] 53-54, n. 93.)

Sometimes a list will use anaphora not to begin each example but to initiate sections of examples. For example, when in *Chance* (*Mor.* 97C-D) Plutarch constructs an example list to argue against the existence of the goddess Fate, he begins each of his three groups of rhetorical questions by repetition of ἐκ τύχης μὲν/δὲ καὶ διὰ τύχην ("Was it the result of chance and because of chance that . . . ?").[18] In so doing he binds the sections together and stresses his point that human decision, not Fate, is the cause of human events. This effectively makes the various examples appear representative of a great many more, all of which would give the same general impression: "Did Fate cause Aristeides [Scipio, Philocrates, Lasthenes and Euthycrates, and Alexander] to perform such and such action? Obviously not; it was due to his own choice."

Similar to this approach used by Plutarch is the manner in which Wisdom 10 begins each section of its list of famous people with αὕτη ("this one" = "she" 10:1a, 5a, 6a, 10a, 13a, and 15a). Through the list the author seeks to demonstrate the truth of the assertion made in 9:18, that Wisdom works in the lives of all those who follow her. The literary connection of the example list to 9:18 is immediately visible in the way 10:1 relies on "Wisdom" (τῇ σοφίᾳ) in 9:18 for the identity of αὕτη. "Translations like the RSV regularly insert the noun "Wisdom" for the convenience of modern readers, but this practice obscures the majestic anaphora of the Greek text as well as the organic connection between chapters 9 and 10.""[19] The first three sections of the list rely upon τῇ σοφίᾳ in 9:18 for the identity of αὕτη, and the second three sections rely on σοφία in 10:9 for the same. Thus, midway through the list the author places a sentence restating the meaning of 9:18c, placing again before the reader what the list is designed to demonstrate: "Wisdom rescued from afflictions those who served her" (Wisdom 10:9).

On several occasions anaphora is used in only part of a list. For example, when meditating on the universal nature of death, Marcus Aurelius

---

[18]Plutarch, *Moralia*, vol. 2, trans. F. C. Babbitt, LCL (New York: G. P. Putnam's Sons, 1928) 75.

[19]J. M. Reese, *The Book of Wisdom, Song of Songs*, OT Message 20 (Wilmington DE: Michael Glazier, Inc., 1983) 109.

lists a series of famous men and asserts that they all died (VI.47). In one section of this list, four successive clauses begin with τοσοῦτοι ("so many"). His anaphora is designed to emphasize the inclusiveness of the examples, and this impression is enhanced with asyndeton in the subsequent listing of people and categories:

> We must pass at last to the same bourne whither *so many* wonderful orators have gone, *so many* grave philosophers, Heraclitus, Pythagoras, Socrates: *so many* heroes of old time, and *so many* warriors, *so many* tyrants of later days. . . . (VI.47, emphasis mine)[20]

Through repetition of "so many," the list emphasizes the fact that "all" die.

Also worthy of mention is Philo's modified use of anaphora to begin rhetorical questions in *Who Is the Heir?* 260-62, where he elucidates the meaning of Genesis 15:12: "And about sunset a trance (ἔκστασις) fell upon Abram." To explain that only righteous people are inspired by God to give prophetic speech in an ecstatic trance, he lists a group of righteous men considered to be prophets. The first, Noah, is explicitly called "righteous," but the next three examples, each beginning with τί δέ, rhetorically imply that Isaac, Jacob and Moses were also righteous prophets: ὁ Νῶε δίκαιος. . . . τί δὲ Ἰσαάκ; τί δὲ Ἰακώβ; . . . τί δὲ Μωϋσης; ("Noah was just. . . . What of Isaac? What of Jacob? . . . What of Moses?").

The dominant use of anaphora in the example lists, to enhance the impression that the examples included are merely representative of a great many more that could also be employed, is not the typical use of anaphora described by the rhetorical handbooks. They explain this rhetorical technique as the repetition of a word at the beginning of successive clauses to increase the impact of a particular point. For example, *Ad Herennium* cites the following:

> *To you* must go the credit for this, *to you* are thanks due, *to you* will this act of yours bring glory. [Repetition of *vobis.*] *You venture* to enter the

---

[20]*The Communings with Himself of Marcus Aurelius Antoninus,* trans. C. R. Haines, LCL (New York: G. P. Putnam's Sons, 1916) 157.

Forum? *You venture* to face the light? *You venture* to come into the sight of these men? *Dare you* say a word? *Dare you* make a request of them? *Dare you* beg off punishment? *What* can you say in your defense? *What* do you dare demand? *What* do you think should be granted to you? *Have you not* violated your oath? *Have you not* betrayed your friends? *Have you not* raised your hand against your father? *Have you not,* I ask, wallowed in every shame? (*Ad Her.* IV.13.19, emphasis mine; anaphoric use of *tu, audes, quid est quod* and *non*)[21]

The force of the shaming argument in the second quotation is intensified by the changing use of anaphors, which are normally used three times each. Quintilian further clarifies this technique with his statement that "a number of clauses may begin with the same word for the sake of force and emphasis."[22] He gives as an example:

Nihilne te nocturnum praesidium Palatii,
nihil urbis vigiliae,
nihil timor populi,
nihil consensus bonorum omnium,
nihil hic munitissimus habendi senatus locus,
nihil horum ora vultusque moverunt?

Were you unmoved by the guard set each night upon the Palatine,
unmoved by the patrolling of the city,
unmoved by the terror of the people,
unmoved by the unanimity of all good citizens,
unmoved by the choice of so strongly fortified a spot for the assembly of
    the senate,
unmoved by the looks and faces of those here present today?

(*Inst. Or.* IX.3.30)[23]

Such implementation of anaphora, while uncommon in the example lists, sometimes does occur. Cicero, when arguing against the division of

---

[21]*Rhetorica ad Herennium,* trans. H. Caplan, LCL (Cambridge: Harvard University Press, 1954) 277. Cf. Quint. IX.3.30 where six rhetorical questions in a row begin with *nihil.*

[22]Quintilian, *Institutio Oratoria,* vol. 3 trans. H. E. Butler, LCL (New York: G. P. Putnam's Sons, 1922) 463.

[23]Ibid.

intellectual disciplines into separate departments, starts three successive statements with *quae de* to magnify the impressiveness of the philosopher Hippias' areas of expertise.

> Hippias . . . boasted . . . that he had not only acquired the accomplishments that form the basis of the liberal education of a gentleman, mathematics, music, knowledge of literature and poetry, and the doctrines of natural science, ethics and political science [quae de naturis rerum, quae de hominum moribus, quae de rebus publicis dicerentur se tenere], but had made with his own hand the ring he had on, the cloak he was dressed in and the boots he was wearing. (*De Oratore* III.127)[24]

This illustrates the truth of his opening comment:

> Crassus, . . . out of what narrow limitations you have been bold enough to rescue the orator and elevate him to the throne of his ancestors! For in the good old days, as we are told, the professors and masters of rhetoric considered no kind of discourse to lie outside their province, and continually occupied themselves with every system of oratory.[25]

Later on, while still arguing against those whom he considers ignorant technicians of rhetoric, mere linguistic manipulators, he employs a similar technique. Asserting that orators need a broad grasp of knowledge in all fields, Cicero uses rhetorical questions which begin with *quid de* and are linked by means of adjunction (reliance of several clauses upon the same verb found either at the beginning or end of the series): "Quid de Prodico Ceo, quid de Thrasymacho Chalcedonio, de Protagora Abderita loquar?" ("What shall I say about Prodicus of Ceos or [what shall I say about] Thrasymachus of Chalcedon or [what shall I say about] Protagorus of Abdera?" III.128)[26] Still hammering away at the same point, in III.132 Cicero begins the three parts of one rhetorical question with *alios qui* and the first three clauses of the next rhetorical question with *num*.

> An tu existimas cum esset Hippocrates ille Cous fuisse tum

---

[24]Cicero, *De Oratore*, vol. 2, trans. H. Rackham, LCL (Cambridge: Harvard University Press, 1942) 99, 101.

[25]Ibid., 99.

[26]Ibid., 101.

alios medicos qui morbis
alios   qui vulneribus
alios   qui oculis mederentur?
num geometriam Euclide aut Archimede
num musicam Damone aut Aristoxeno
num ipsas litteras Aristophane aut
Callimacho tractante tam discerptas fuisse ut nemo genus universum
    plecteretur . . . ?

Do you really suppose that in the time of the great Hippocrates of Cos there
    were some physicians who specialized in medicine and others in sur-
    gery and others in ophthalmic cases? or that mathematics in the hands
    of Euclid or Archimedes, or music with Damon or Aristoxenus, or even
    literature with Aristophanes or Callimachus were such entirely separate
    subjects that nobody embraced culture as a whole, . . . ?[27]

One may observe by these examples, therefore, that the common rhetorical use of anaphora is not the kind used in most of the example lists.
Anaphora is generally employed in them as a magnification technique,
along with other rhetorical devices used for the same end. And by far the
most effective implementation of anaphora for this purpose is found in Hebrews 11:3-31.

---

[27]Ibid., 103. Similarly, in 139 Cicero uses anaphora in several rhetorical questions to
demonstrate how past orators received philosophical training. Each example either begins
with *aliis* or implies its presence through the use of *aut*.

Aliisne . . . Dionem instituit Plato?

aliis Isocrates . . . Timotheum?

aut aliis Pythagoreus ille Lysis Thebanum Epaminondam?

aut Xenophon Agesilaum?

aut Philolaus Archytam Tarentinum?

aut ipse Pythagoras . . . ?

One might also notice that Plutarch begins *Chance* with anaphoric use of οὐδέ to link together four human virtues in the opening question: πότερον οὐδὲ δικαιοσύνη τὰ θνητῶν
πράγματα οὐδ' ἰσότης οὐδὲ σωφροσύνη οὐδὲ κοσμιότης . . . ; ("Is it true that
man's ways are not justice either, or equality, or self-control, or decorum?").

Chapter 5

Rhetorical Composition
of Hebrews 11:32-40

Asyndeton and Isocolon in Hebrews 11:32-34

A major transition occurs at Hebrews 11:32 where the anaphoric use of πίστει and the recounting of examples of specific people cease. Yet the rhetorical magnification effect of anaphora in 11:3-31 is continued by other techniques in 11:32-38. While differing substantially from 11:3-31 on a compositional level, this second part of the list has largely the same rhetorical function.

With the termination of the πίστει series, strictly chronological arrangement is also abandoned. For example, the actual chronological order presented in the biblical narrative for the figures listed in verse 32 is Barak (Judges 4:6ff.), Gideon (Judges 6:11ff.), Jephthah (Judges 11:1ff.), Samson (Judges 13:2ff.), Samuel (1 Samuel 1:20ff.) and David (1 Samuel 16:12ff.), whereas this verse lists them: Gideon, Barak, Samson, Jephthah, David, and Samuel. Hebrews 11:32-38 *alludes* to the careers of faithful servants of God in a loosely chronological progression, and the allusions are not limited to biblical figures. Commentators have long recognized that the author's statements include references to people and events from the Maccabees and the Martyrdom of Isaiah.[1] Providing a brief

---

[1]E.g., Owen, 7:196ff. (also Westcott, 381ff.; Moffatt, 186ff.; Windisch, 105-106; Michel, 418-20; Spicq, 364ff.; Montefiore, 208ff.; Bruce, 331ff.; and Buchanan, 203ff.; etc.).

glimpse of a great sweep of salvation history, the goal of this section is to give *impressions* of faith-inspired heroism, and this goal is greatly enhanced by several rhetorical techniques.

The transition from 11:3-31 is made by employing a rhetorical question followed by a claim that time and space do not allow continued recounting of examples: καὶ τί ἔτι λέγω; ἐπιλείψει με γὰρ διηγούμενον ὁ χρόνος περὶ Γεδεών . . . ("What shall I yet say? For time does not allow me to tell about Gideon . . . "). Although some commentators do briefly mention that this is a rhetorical technique, they say little about why or how it is used. Michel, for example, calls it a rhetorical art of interruption and adds that it was a well-known form, citing as evidence some examples of its use in Philo.[2] Spicq provides perhaps the most detailed list of parallels;[3] and since these parallels verify the fact that Hebrews 11:32 reflects a widely recognized rhetorical technique, it is somewhat surprising that only one of the other twenty-five example lists employs it. This occurs when Isocrates concludes the main body of his list by saying, "But we should both grow weary, you with listening and I with speaking, if we were to examine every incident of this sort" (*Archidamus* 47).[4]

---

[2]Michel, 415 n. 1: Philo, *Life of Moses* I.213; *On the Sacrifices of Abel and Cain* 27; *Special Laws* IV.238; *Somn.* II.63; and *Leg. ad Gaium* 323. Michel also cites P. Wendland, *Urchristliche Literaturformen* (3rd ed., 1912) 373; E. Riggenbach, *Kommentar*, introduction, xiv; and Blass and Debrunner, §366. Other scholars who mention that Heb 11:32 is a rhetorical technique include Windisch, 105 ("einer bekannten rhetorischen Formel"); Moffatt, 184, who gives examples and Greek quotations and says, "καὶ τί ἔτι λέγω . . . was a literary as well as an oratorical phrase" (cf. Josephus, *Ant.* XX.11.1). "Ἐπιλείψει γάρ . . . is one form of a common rhetorical phrase, though ἡ ἡμέρα is generally used instead of ὁ χρόνος." Bruce, 330, calls it "a rhetorical transition" and cites *Ant.* XX.11.257.

[3]For καὶ τί ἔτι λέγω; in Heb 11:32, he cites Josephus, *Ant.* XX.11.256 (καὶ τί δεῖ πλείω λέγειν); and for ἐπιλείψει με γὰρ διηγούμενον ὁ χρόνος . . . in Heb 11:32 he cites as parallels Athenaeus, V.63 (ἐπιλείποι δ' ἄν με πᾶς χρόνος . . .); Livy, XXVIII.41; Cicero, *Pro Sext. Rosc.* XXXII.89 ("Tempus hercule, me citius quam oratio deficeret"); Dion. of Halicarnassus, *De compos. verb.* 4; Demosthenes, *Pro coron.* 296; Philo, *De somm.* II.263 (ἐπιλείψει με ἡ ἡμέρα . . .); *De sacrif. Abel. et Caini* 27 (ἐπιλείψει με ἡ ἡμέρα λέγοντα τὰ τῶν κατ' εἶδος ἀρετῶν ὀνόματα;); *De spec. leg.* IV.238; *De Vit. Mos.* I.213; and *De Virt.* 101 (Spicq, 2:362). See also Westcott, 378, and Moffatt, 184, for Greek quotations.

[4]*Isocrates*, vol. 1, trans. G. Norlin, LCL (New York: G. P. Putnam's Sons, 1928) 373.

The rhetorical function of Hebrews 11:32 is to begin to bring an already lengthy list to a conclusion and yet give the impression that the author could go on piling up ever more examples of similar content. The direct appeal to lack of time in 11:32a is rhetorically enhanced by employing asyndeton (omission of conjunctions) in the list of names in 11:32b and actions in 11:33-34.

32. Καὶ τί ἔτι λέγω;
    ἐπιλείψει με γὰρ διηγούμενον ὁ χρόνος περὶ   Γεδεών,
                                   Βαράκ,
                                   Σαμψών,
                                   Ἰεφθάε,
                                   Δαυίδ
                                   τε καὶ Σαμουὴλ
                                   καὶ τῶν προφητῶν,

33. οἳ διὰ πίστεως   κατηγωνίσαντο βασιλείας,
                      εἰργάσαντο δικαιοσύνην,
                      ἐπέτυχον ἐπαγγελιῶν,
                      ἔφραξαν στόματα λεόντων,
34.   ἔσβεσαν δύναμιν πυρός,
                      ἔφυγον στόματα μαχαίρης,
                      ἐδυναμώθησαν ἀπὸ ἀσθενείας,
                      ἐγενήθησαν ἰσχυροὶ ἐν πολέμῳ,
                      παρεμβολὰς ἔκλιναν ἀλλοτρίων.

32. And what more need I say?
    For time fails me to tell about Gideon,
                      Barak,
                      Samson,
                      Jephthah,
                      David,
                      and Samuel,
                      and the prophets,
33. who through faith conquered kingdoms,
                      worked righteousness,
                      received promises,
                      stopped mouths of lions,
34.   extinguished raging fire,
                      fled mouths of swords,
                      were strengthened from weakness,
                      became mighty in war,
                      put armies of others to flight.

The value of asyndeton for the author of Hebrews may be seen clearly in Quintilian's statement that asyndeton "is useful when we are speaking with special vigour: for it at once impresses the details on the mind and makes them *seem more numerous than they really are*" (IX.3.50 emphasis mine).[5] Of both asyndeton and its sister technique polysyndeton (use of many conjunctions) Quintilian says that "they make our utterances more vigorous and emphatic and produce an impression of vehemence such as might spring from repeated outbursts of emotion" (IX.3.54).[6] Although this type of emotional barrage is more intense than what one would expect from reading Hebrews 11:32-34, the author of Hebrews does employ asyndeton to make his examples "seem more numerous than they really are."

Because the clauses in verses 33-34 are of equivalent length and structure, they form an example of isocolon, which *Ad Her.* IV.20.27 defines as follows:

> We call Isocolon the figure comprised of cola which consist of a virtually equal number of syllables. To effect the isocolon we shall not count the syllables—for that is surely childish—but experience and practice will bring such a facility that by a sort of instinct we can produce again a colon of equal length to the one before it. . . . In this figure it may often happen that the number of syllables seems equal without being precisely so—as when one colon is shorter than the other by one or even two syllables, or when one colon contains more syllables, and the other contains one or more longer or fuller-sounding syllables, so that the length or fullness of sound of these matches and counterbalances the greater number of syllables in the other.[7]

This rhetorical handbook specifies that "Colon or clause is the name given to a sentence member, brief and complete, which does not express the en-

---

[5] *The Institutio Oratoria of Quintilian*, vol. 3, trans. H. E. Butler, LCL (Cambridge: Harvard University Press, 1922) 475.

[6] Ibid., 477. See also *Ad Her.* IV.30.41 and Arist., *Rhet.* III.12.2-4; 19.6 where Aristotle says asyndeton finds effective use at the end of an oration; and Dem., *On Style* 61-62.

[7] *Rhetorica Ad Herennium*, trans. H. Caplan, LCL (Cambridge: Harvard University Press, 1954) 295.

tire thought, but is in turn supplemented by another colon'' (*Ad Her.* IV.19.26).[8] It is interesting to note, therefore, that in Hebrews 11:33-34 each of the clauses is dependent upon οἱ διὰ πίστεως in 11:33a as its subject; and as a group these clauses combine to finish the thought begun in 11:32b with the onset of the list of names.

While the clauses of 11:33-34 represent an example of isocolon, the string of names in 11:32b represents another rhetorical technique that adds a slightly different dimension. Hebrews 11:32b represents what *Ad Her.* IV.19.26 calls a comma: "It is called a Comma or Phrase when single words are set apart by pauses in staccato speech, as follows : 'By your vigour, voice, looks you have terrified your adversaries.'"[9] The difference between the comma of 11:32b and the isocolon of 11:33-34 reveals a subtle rhetorical distinction between these two subsets. *Ad Herennium* makes the distinction very clear when it specifies that

> There is this difference in onset between the last figure [comma] and the one preceding [colon]: the former moves upon its object more slowly and less often, the latter strikes more quickly and frequently. Accordingly in the first figure it seems that the arm draws back and the hand whirls about to bring the sword to the adversary's body, while in the second his body is as it were pierced with quick and repeated thrusts.[10]

In Hebrews 11:32b the author delivers a quick, stabbing verbal attack on the ears of his listeners, and then he slows down slightly in 11:33-34 to deliver slashes with his verbal sword. The resulting rapidly rhythmic barrage of names and accomplishments enhances the explicit claim of verse 32b, giving the impression that great numbers of people crowd into the author's mind as he speaks. The lives of an overwhelming number of men and women are potentially available for use as examples of how faith motivates those whom God commends.

Accenting this use of asyndeton and isocolon is a form of sound repetition in verses 33-34. There is a striking use of aorist verbs at the begin-

---

[8]Ibid., 293.

[9]Ibid., 295.

[10]Ibid., 297.

ning of these phrases so that verses 33b-34d all begin with a similar sound due to the augment ἐ.[11] In addition, there is a chiastic ordering of the endings of these aorist verbs: 33a-b end with σαντο, followed by the second aorist ending ον in 33c; 33d-34a both end in a sibilant (σαν) sound and form the middle of the set; 34b, like 33c, ends in ον, so that the middle two verbs in 33d-34a are preceded and followed by second aorist verbs; and 34c-d end in θησαν. Thus there is for 33a-34d a chiastic patterning of the initial aorist verb endings that enhances the "e" sound of the augments and the rhetorical effect of asyndeton.

> κατηγωνίσαντο . . .
> εἰργάσαντο . . .
> ἐπέτυχον . . .
> ἔφραξαν . . .
> ἔσβεσαν . . .
> ἔφυφον . . .
> ἐδυναμώθησαν . . .
> ἐλενήθησαν . . .

The final phrase (verse 34e) alters the sequence of words, placing the verb in the second position; and this breaking of the pattern signals the conclusion of the series.[12]

The combination of phrases of equal length strung together without conjunctions in 11:33-34, most beginning with a distinct "e" sound, and as a group having a chiastic verb ending pattern, creates a definite rhythm

---

[11]See Aristotle, *Rhet.* III.9.9 for a classification of sound repetition that discusses beginnings and endings of words.

[12]Michel, 415, arranges the clauses of 11:33-34 into three groups, noting that they have a poetic structure.

> 1. κατηγωνίσαντο βασιλείας,   2. ἔφραξαν στόματα λεόντων,
>   ἠργάσαντο δικαιοσύην,   ἔσβεσαν δύναμιν πύρος,
>   ἐπέτυχον ἐπαγγελιῶν,   ἔφυγον στόματα μαχαίρης,
>
>   3. ἐδυναμώθησαν ἀπὸ ἀσθενείας,
>   ἐγενήθησαν ἰσχυροι ἐν πολέμω
>   παρεμβολὰς ἔκλιναν ἀλλοτρίων.

He postulates that they might have comprised a formerly independent unit on victories in war (416).

in oral presentation. The resulting oral artistry enhances the author's desired impression that the number of people and actions to which he alludes is immense.[13]

The staccato stabbing and slashing of verses 32-34 penetrates the minds of the listeners with success stories: these people subdued kings, shut the mouths of lions, put foreign armies to flight, and were made strong in weakness. Yet this is only the shiny side of the coin. The dull flip side, which applies more appropriately to those to whom this sermon was addressed, is presented in verses 35b-38.[14] The still positive note of verse 35a, of women receiving their dead back to life, is shattered by a different sound at the beginning of verse 35b: ἄλλοι δέ, "But others. . . ."[15]

The hideous things suffered by those to whom the author alludes in verses 35-38 are not presented with the same stereotyped clausal structure employed in verses 33-34.[16] Yet after the initial comments in verses 35b-36, the staccato stabbing of the ears does in fact return with the piling up of descriptive words and phrases without connecting particles in verse 37. The rhetorical effect of this particular series is enhanced by the repetition of the aorist passive ending θησαν in verse 37a-b, the use of the particle ἐν three times in verse 37c-e, and the repetition of the participle ending ομενοι in verse 37f-h.

ἐλιθάσθησαν,
ἐπρίσθησαν,
ἐν φόνῳ μαχαίρης ἀπέθανον,

---

[13]Vanhoye, 192, notes that the rhythm of 11:33-35a is very carefully accomplished to give a sense of amplification, and even a clumsy translation allows perception of this. He further comments that the rhythm of vv. 35b-38 is more varied, beginning slowly with an explanation, then distinctly accelerating in v. 37 where several verbs are used without complements or conjunctions; and without loss of power prepositions take over from the verbs, followed by four participles without conjunctions.

[14]Spicq, 2: 362, separates 11:32-38 into "great actions" (11:32-35a) and "great sufferings" (11:35b-38).

[15]See "Antithesis" below in ch. 6 for a discussion of the contrast.

[16]Vanhoye, 192, provides an interesting comment on these verses. See above, n. 13, for details.

περιῆλθον ἐν μηλωταῖς,
            ἐν αἰγείοις δέρμασιν,
ὑστερούμενοι
θλιβόμενοι
κακουχούμενοι. . . .

They were stoned;
they were sawn (in two);
they were murdered by the sword;
they went around in sheepskin,
            in the skin of goats,
being in need,
being afflicted,
being tormented. . . .

Although these faithful people suffered atrocities for their courage, they are examples of heroic faithfulness just as much as those who put foreign armies to flight.[17]

Hebrews 11:38 offers a brief commentary on these suffering faithful, calling them those ''of whom the world was not worthy.'' Instead of stressing their homeless plight by yet another use of asyndeton, however, in verse 38 the author employs polysyndeton, connecting verse 38c-e with three uses of the conjunction καί. The effect is essentially the same as the previous use of asyndeton. Using καί to string together four descriptions of nonsettled existence, the wandering condition of the faithful is stressed by culminating the series with the bleak phrase ''and holes in the ground.''

38. ὧν οὐκ ἦν ἄξιος ὁ κόσμος,
        ἐπὶ ἐρημίαις πλανώμενοι
        καὶ ὄρεσιν
        καὶ σπηλαίοις
        καὶ ταῖς ὀπαῖς τῆς γῆς.

38. of whom the world was not worthy,
        wandering upon deserts,
        and mountains,
        and caves,
        and holes in the ground.

---

[17]See Spicq, 2:369-71 for an excursus on ''the better resurrection.''

These people whom the world persecuted and killed, who were forced to wander through deserts and live in mountains and caves and holes in the ground (verse 38), these whom the world rejected are models of faith of whose presence the world was not worthy. The staccato verbalization of terms and phrases emphasizes both the magnitude of their suffering and the number of those who suffered.

For those Christians addressed by the author who are suffering discouragement and contemplating apostasy, the example list is designed to instill bravery. The specific examples of men and women from the earliest times through the conquest of Jericho and the summary of great accomplishments and great sufferings of people from the times of the Judges up through the Maccabean era provide a ringing call to bravery in the present time. In 11:1-31 anaphora is the dominant rhetorical technique, providing continuity of content by centering every example on the topic of faith. The anaphoric πίστει gives a sense of rhythm to the otherwise fairly diverse set of examples and enhances the impression that a multitude of similar examples could be added to prove the author's point. This impression of immensity is explicitly stated in verse 32a-b and then given further emphasis through asyndeton, isocolon, paronomasia, and polysyndeton in verses 32c-38.

When forcefully delivered in oral presentation, the entire list presents an intensely emotional appeal. The audience is made to realize that in their suffering they have joined a host of God's people who have gone before them. This is soon given explicit formulation when the author summarizes his point in 12:1, "Therefore, since we are surrounded by so great a cloud of witnesses. . . . " The magnitude of any present suffering is overshadowed by what the faithful of the past endured, for the author's listeners have not yet resisted to the point of shedding their blood (12:4).

Polysyndeton and Asyndeton in Other Example Lists

Although asyndeton rarely occurs in the other example lists, polysyndeton regularly is used, and generally its rhetorical function is to make the number of examples seem more impressive, especially in the shorter lists. Several lists rely heavily on polysyndeton to make their brief contents appear all inclusive. In Aristotle, *Rhetoric* II.23.11, the examples are united with καί, and there is a stereotyped, repeated clausal structure in which the clauses are further united by the use of adjunction (the reliance upon one verb of all the clauses in a series; in this case "honored"). Together these techniques help create the impression that talented people everywhere are honored, regardless of their positions.

Πάριοι γοῦν Ἀρχίλοχον καίπερ βλάσφημον ὄντα τετιμήκασι,
καὶ Χῖοι Ὅμηρον οὐκ ὄντα πολιτικόν,
καὶ Μυτιληναῖοι Σαπφὼ καίπερ γυναῖκα οὖσαν,
καὶ Λακεδαιμόνιοι Χίλωνα . . .
καὶ Ἰταλιῶται Πυθαγόραν,
καὶ Λαμψακηνοὶ Ἀναξαγόραν ξένον ὄντα ἔθαψαν καὶ τιμῶσιν.

Parians honoured Archilochus, in spite of his blasphemy,
and Chians Homer, although he was not politically active,
and Mytilenaeans Sappho, although she was a woman,
and Lacedaemonians Chilon . . .
and Italiotes Pythagoras,
and Lampsacenes Anaxagoras, although he was an alien, they buried and
      still honor him.[18]

On a smaller scale, Cicero combines polysyndeton with adjunction to give added weight to the five realms in which the expertise of three famous orators was sought.

ut ad eos de omnibus divinis atque
humanis rebus referrtur
eidemque et in senatu
            et apud populum
            et in causis amicorum
            et domi
            et militiae consilium suum fidemque praestabant.

about every kind of matter, both divine and secular, they were consulted,
and in the senate,
and in the civic assembly,
and in lawsuits of friends,
and at home,

---

[18]Because the rhetorical techniques that so dominate the composition of this list are omitted in the English translation of the Loeb volume (Aristotle, *The "Art" of Rhetoric,* trans. J. H. Freese, LCL [New York: G. P. Putnam's Sons, 1926] 307), I have provided a more literal version.

and in foreign service they employed their wisdom and loyalty.

(*De Oratore* III.134)[19]

Perhaps the most striking use of polysyndeton in the example lists is in 4 Ezra, where Ezra is questioning the angelic revealer on the justice of God's refusing to hear intercessory prayer at the last judgment. Presenting a list of famous individuals who prayed for people in the past, he combines polysyndeton with repetition of clausal format to make his examples appear representative of a great many other cases that could also be cited of prayers by the righteous.

> How is it that . . . Abraham prayed for the people of Sodom,
> and Moses for our fathers who sinned in the wilderness;
> and Joshua after him for Israel in the days of Achar;
> and Samuel in the days of Saul,
> and David for the plague,
> and Solomon for those that (should worship) in the sanctuary;
> and Elijah for those who received the rain
> and   for the dead, that they might live;
> and Hezekiah for the people in the days of Sennacherib,
> and (others) many for many?[20]

In the longer lists polysyndeton is used in more limited ways. Isocrates, for example, employs it to emphasize the insignificance of Dionysius's birth and background by connecting descriptive phrases with καί in *To Philip* 65.[21]

---

[19]Again, because the translation in *De Oratore, Books I-III*, trans. E. W. Sutton, LCL (Cambridge: Harvard University Press, 1942) 105, does not reveal the use of polysyndeton, I have given a more literal rendering. For another instance of polysyndeton, see also the text quoted in ch. 4 above, where Marcus Aurelius combines polysyndeton with anaphoric use of τοσοῦτοι (so many) to emphasize the immense numbers of people to whom he refers (VI.47).

[20]Trans. G. H. Box, in the *The Apocrypha and Pseudepigrapha of the Old Testament in English*, vol. 2, ed. R. H. Charles (Oxford: Clarendon Press, 1913).

[21]I have again provided a more literal translation than that found in the Loeb edition, *Isocrates*, 1.285. Note also that in *Archidamus* 45 Isocrates uses conjunctions to heighten the contrast when describing events in the life of Dionysius.

πολλοστὸς ὢν Συρακοσίων καὶ τῷ γένει
καὶ τῇ δόξῃ
καὶ τοῖς ἄλλοις ἅπασιν.

Being the least among the Syracusans, even in birth,
                              and in reputation
                              and in all other matters.

Asyndeton, which is important in Hebrews 11:32-34, is found less frequently than polysyndeton in the example lists. M. Aurelius, for example, uses it to enhance the power of a lengthy list of specific individuals and categories of people.

ἐπὶ τούτοις δὲ Εὔδοξος,
            Ἵππαρχος,
            Ἀρχιμήδης,
            ἄλλαι φύσεις ὀξεῖαι,
            μεγαλόφρονες,
            φιλόπονοι,
            πανοῦργοι,
            αὐθάδεις,
            αὐτῆς τῆς ἐπικήου
            καὶ ἐφημέρου τῶν ἀνθρώπων ζωῆς χλευασταί,
            οἷον Μένιππος
            καὶ ὅσοι τοιοῦτοι.

. . . and besides them, Eudoxus, Hipparchus, Archimedes, and other acute natures, men of large minds, lovers of toil, men of versatile powers, men of strong will, mockers like Menippus and many other such.

(*Meditations* VI.47)[22]

Interestingly, this use of asyndeton balances Aurelius's use of anaphora and polysyndeton in his list immediately prior to this passage (see above in chapter 4). Thus, it is similar to the use of both asyndeton and polysyndeton in Hebrews 11:32-38.

A final case of asyndeton is found in 1 Clement 5:6-7a, where it is used within one example to increase the impressive sound of the list of sufferings endured and accomplishments made by the apostle Paul.

---

[22]*The Communings with Himself of Marcus Aurelius Antoninus*, trans. C. R. Haines, LCL (New York: G. P. Putnam's Sons, 1916) 157.

. . . seven times he was in bonds,
>   he was exiled,
>   he was stoned,
>   he was a herald both in the East and in the West,
>   he gained the noble fame of his faith,
>   he taught righteousness to all the world.[23]

Thus, the example lists employ polysyndeton and asyndeton either as devices of central importance to their overall structure or as magnification techniques in smaller segments. Either way they are designed to make their evidence seem more abundant than it really is.

Stereotyped Clausal Structure in Example Lists

Example lists that are rather brief tend to indicate universality of representation rhetorically by repeating the same clausal structure in each example. When only a very limited amount is recorded about each person, the tendency is to present each example with approximately the same formula. Primarily this is a phenomenon of Jewish lists. In 1 Maccabees 2:50-64, where Mattathias uses examples to exhort his sons to remain faithful to Torah, all but one of his examples use the following format: the name of the Jewish worthy plus ἐν τῷ/τῇ plus an infinitive or dative noun plus a description of the man's action plus a statement about the man's reward for faithfulness (for example, "Joshua, because he fulfilled the command, became a judge in Israel" 2:55).[24] Similarly, in 4 Maccabees 18:10-19,

---

[23]*The Apostolic Fathers,* vol. 1, trans. Kirsopp Lake, LCL (Cambridge: Harvard University Press, 1912) 17.

[24]This particular use of ἐν with an articular infinitive is unusual. Constructions of this kind in the NT occur primarily in Luke, usually in a temporal sense meaning "while." Blass and Debrunner point out that ἐν τῷ σπείρειν αὐτον in Matt 13:4, for example, is equivalent to the classical σπείροντος αὐτοῦ. They observe that Attic does not use ἐν τῷ in this manner, but the LXX often does so in translating the Hebrew ב plus infinitive, a construction not found in Aramaic (*A Greek Grammar of the New Testament and Other Early Christian Literature,* trans. and ed. R. W. Funk [Chicago: University of Chicago Press, 1961] 208, §404). Most likely this Hebrew construction lies behind the Greek translation of the cause and effect sentences in 1 Macc 2:54-56, 58 with ἐν τῷ carrying the instrumental meaning "because" (ibid). The same meaning is generated in vv. 57 and

where the valiant Jewish mother is exhorting her sons to face martyrdom bravely, the first section of references to her husband's teaching in 18:12-14 has a stereotyped structure: an aorist verb plus a conjunction plus the situation encountered plus the name of the person (for example, ἐδόχαζεν δὲ καὶ τὸν ἐν λάκκῳ λεόντων Δανιηλ, ὃν ἐμακάριζεν, "He praised Daniel in the den of lions and blessed him" 18:13).[25] Ezra's case for intercessory prayer in 4 Ezra 7:106-10 is also composed with the general format: "and" plus the name of person who prayed plus "for" plus the matter about which the person prayed (see text above).

In Greco-Roman literature the only list presenting its examples with stereotyped clausal format occurs in Aristotle's *Rhetoric* II.23.11. The brief statements made about each person in the list all have the following sequence: καί plus the name of the nation honoring the person plus name of the person they honored plus the reason why this honor should be considered unexpected (see text above). As seen previously, this repeated format is combined with polysyndeton and adjunction to increase the persuasive

---

60, which have ἐν τῷ/τῇ plus a dative noun, and this construction also reflects Hebrew syntax. Similar instances of such instrumental uses may be seen in Acts 7:29 where Stephen says, ἔφυγεν δὲ Μωϋσῆς ἐν τῷ λόγῳ τούτῳ, and Matt 6:7 where Jesus asserts that the Gentiles think that they will be heard ἐν τῇ πολυλογίᾳ αὐτῶν (cf. Heb 2:18; Acts 24:16; Rom 8:3) (Maximilan Zerwick, *Biblical Greek,* trans. J. Smith [Rome: Scripta Pontificii Instituti Biblici, 1963] 40, §89). Ἐν τῷ plus the articular infinitive and ἐν τῷ plus the dative noun in 1 Macc 2:54-60 reflect two Hebrew expressions of instrumental meaning, and the structure of all these verses is essentially the same. Only v. 59 stands out as an exception in vv. 54-60, and here the use of the aorist participle πιστεύσαντες carries the meaning "because they believed." Consequently, from 54-60 all of the examples employ the same syntactical sequence: Name plus because of (his action or quality of character) plus was rewarded by God.

1 Macc 2:51 and 52, on the other hand, employ ἐν plus a dative noun in the sense of "when": "Abraham, when he was tested. . . . Joseph, during the time of his distress. . . . " These two examples also vary from the others in that they begin their effect clauses with καί. But in spite of these differences, they still put forward the same general structure of name plus virtuous action plus reward by God.

[25]The first three examples are joined by adjunction so that the format of the first example is transposed, and the second and third rely on the latter part of the first for their initial component parts (ἀνεγίνωσκέν τε ὑμῖν).

quality of the list in demonstrating that talented people are everywhere honored.[26]

Conclusion: Hebrews 11:39-40

In 11:39-40 the author of Hebrews brings his example list to a conclusion. Although not a formal conclusion of great rhetorical power, it nevertheless summarizes and brings to a climax the preceding material. Vanhoye points out that by calling attention to the divine commendation for the faith of all of those in the example list, verse 39 echoes the introductory comments in verse 2 as well as the examples of Abel and Enoch in verses 4 and 5.[27] It also concludes the summary section of the list, 11:32-38, by resuming the formula used at the beginning of verse 33: διὰ πίστεως. In addition, by saying that none of the people mentioned has as yet obtained *the* promise, verse 39 indicates that the comment in verse 33, "they received promises," is only a partial fulfillment and not to be confused with the final realization.[28]

All of the faithful down through the ages must wait for God to bring earthly matters to a consummation, and together with the last-time Christians they will all reach the ultimate goal at the same time (verse 40). Thus, the "something better" of verse 40 corresponds with the "better resurrection" of verse 35c, a reward which is reserved for the "better covenant" (8:6; 7:22).[29] According to Vanhoye, the author feels no need to make a direct allusion to the "greater riches" in verse 26 or the "reward" in verse 6, although they are certainly in his mind as he speaks of attaining the promise in verse 39 and "something better" in verse 40. The author does,

---

[26]Other instances of repetition of clausal structure are more limited in scope than in the lists just cited. Cicero combines clausal format repetition in *De Oratore* III.132 with anaphora in listing the different fields of expertise of Hippocrates, and immediately afterward gives three examples of Euclid, Damon, and Aristophanes by combining anaphora and repeated format. In the same list, in III.133, Cicero twice more imploys the same method. (Cf. M. Aurelius III.3.1 on the deaths of Democritus and Socrates.)

[27]Vanhoye, 184, 194.

[28]Ibid., 193.

[29]Ibid., 194.

however, specifically allude to verse 13: "they all died without receiving the promises." And the transition from the plural "promises" to the singular "promise," is, according to Vanhoye, a progression in thought made possible by the reasoning of verses 13-16. Verse 16 specifies that the "better" homeland the patriarchs expected is located in heaven, and this specification makes clear the meaning of "something better" in verse 40.[30] Vanhoye summarizes as follows.

> Thus, this brief phrase (verses 39-40) is presented as the summary of all the important points of the section. By our reckoning the author was not content merely to recount some scenes from the Bible. Certainly the structure of his development is less rigorous here than in other sections, but it is a conclusion nevertheless. The narration of deeds is lucidly organized in the way in which it illuminates the great list as a lesson. Both the positive phase of earthly success stories of faith and the negative phase of those who suffered for their faith are the accomplishments of God.

> In this conclusion the author remarks that *we* also are involved (verse 40). The introduction of the pronoun "we" into the text constitutes an innovation on his part, for it prepares the reader for the following section (12:1-13).[31]

After having composed all of chapter 11 in third person descriptions, with the exception of verse 3, the author in verse 40 reverts back to first person, applying the example list to his listeners by the use of ἡμῶν. This makes the transition back to the language of exhortation that characterizes 10:19-39 and is resumed in 12:1.

In spite of the great bravery and faithfulness exhibited by God's faithful men and women in the past, they will have to wait for the present generation of Christians before they can enter into God's promised rest in the heavenly city (11:10, 13), which is termed in verse 40 the "better" state of perfection.[32] Although commended because of their faith (their tena-

---

[30]Ibid.

[31]Ibid.

[32]See G. Delling, τελειόω, *TDNT,* 8:79, for a convenient and substantial bibliography on perfection in Hebrews. The most current monograph on this subject is a published dissertation by David Peterson, *Hebrews and Perfection: An Examination of the Concept of Perfection in the "Epistle to the Hebrews"* (Cambridge: Cambridge University Press, 1982).

cious belief in future realities that are invisible to physical eyes), not one received the promise for which he or she lived and died in expectation. Consequently, the conclusion in verses 39-40 to a certain degree forms a kind of shaming argument.

The author's listeners have experienced some loss of property, imprisonment, and physical abuse (Hebrews 10:32-35), but these are mild compared to the suffering endured by the heroes of the faith in 11:36-38. The saints of former times exhibited great bravery in spite of the few indications they had of the surety of eternal reward. By comparison, the author's listeners have far greater assurance, since Jesus had come and explained these things in detail. Valiant men and women in the past endured on far less reason for hope, and God has made them wait on those who are privileged to live at the end of the ages. They must wait to experience the eschatological perfection and final rest of the people of God. Watching and waiting, their presence provides great incentive for determined endurance through whatever persecution one may experience. Thus the exhortation following the example list builds upon this excursus into salvation history: "Therefore, since we are surrounded by such a great cloud of witnesses, let us throw off everything that hinders and the sin that so easily entangles, and let us run with perseverance the race marked out for us" (12:1, NIV).

Chapter 6

Antithesis, Hyperbole, Paronomasia, and Circumlocution

Antithesis

In Hebrews 11 and the other such lists the function of the examples is to draw a comparison or contrast between the behavior of each exemplary person and the situation addressed by the speaker. To accomplish this effectively, sometimes the example lists implement the rhetorical technique of antithesis, the placing of contrary statements in juxtaposition to each other. Although its formal use is limited to the Greco-Roman lists formulated by professional rhetoricians, the drawing of contrasts is not uncommon, and Hebrews 11 also uses this technique.

Aristotle's *Rhetoric* provides an explanation of the proper use of antithesis and gives the following example of how to formulate one: "For some of them perished miserably, others saved themselves disgracefully" (*Rhet.* III.9.7).[1] He commends it highly "because contraries are easily understood and even more so when placed side by side, and also because antithesis resembles a syllogism; for refutation is a bringing together of contraries" (*Rhet.* III.9.8).[2] *Ad Herennium* IV.25 calls this technique *con-*

---

[1] Aristotle, *Rhetoric*, trans. J. H. Freese, LCL (New York: G. P. Putnam's Sons, 1926) 393.

[2] Ibid.

tentio, giving as an example: "Flattery has pleasant beginnings, but also brings on bitterest endings."[3]

The author of Hebrews paves the way for his example list in chapter 11 by concluding his exhortation in 10:39 with a strong contrast, ἡμεῖς δὲ οὐκ ἐσμὲν ὑποστολῆς εἰς ἀπώλειαν ἀλλὰ πίστεως εἰς περιποίησιν ψυχῆς ("but we are not of timidity unto destruction but of faith unto preservation of the soul"). And, in keeping with the fact that faith in Hebrews is a tenacious belief in unseen realities, all but one of the antithetical statements within Hebrews 11 focus on the seen and unseen realms of existence. Indeed, the first example juxtaposes the visible and the invisible: μὴ ἐκ φαινομένων τὸ βλεπόμενον γεγονέναι ("not from things which are visible did that which is seen come to be," 11:3). Similarly, 11:9-10 strongly contrasts the transient condition of Abraham in the land God promised to him with the permanent residence he expected in heaven: παρῴκησεν εἰς γῆν τῆς ἐπαγγελίας ὡς ἀλλοτρίαν ἐν σκηναῖς κατοικήσας . . . ἐξεδέχετο γὰρ τὴν τοὺς θεμελίους ἔχουσαν πόλιν ἧς τεχνίτης καὶ δημιουργὸς ὁ θεός ("he sojourned in the land of promise as a foreigner dwelling in tents . . . for he looked forward to the city which has foundations, whose builder and maker is God").

Hebrews 11:24-25 contrasts the suffering of God's people, in which Moses chose to participate, with the pleasures of a royal life in Egypt he had as the son of Pharaoh's daughter. Two earthly lives are contrasted here. Moses rejected the first, a life dominated by an earthly focus and called "the transitory enjoyment of sin" (11:25b). The second, which results from a rejection of the first and involves a sharing in the mistreatment of God's people, ends in the "nontransitory" reward of permanent rest in the heavenly city. Complementing this, Heb 11:26 powerfully asserts the ultimate worth of living for Christ by contrasting the wealth of Egypt with the reproach of Christ: μείζονα πλοῦτον ἡγησάμενος τῶν Αἰγύπτου θησαυρῶν τὸν ὀνειδισμὸν τοῦ Χριστοῦ, ἀπέβλεπεν γὰρ εἰς τὴν

---

[3]*Rhetorica ad Herennium,* trans. Harry Caplan, LCL (Cambridge: Harvard University Press, 1937) 283. Quint. IX.3.81 says that it can occur when single words, pairs of words or sentences are contrasted.

μισθαποδοσίαν·[4]("'he considered the reproach of Christ to be greater wealth than the treasures of Egypt, for he looked [ahead] to the reward'").

In addition to these antithetical statements, there are other contrasts drawn in Hebrews 11. All of 11:35b-38 forms a lengthy contrast with the preceding material in 11:32-35a. Whereas verses 32-35a summarize successful actions accomplished through faith, verses 35b-38 provide a summary of the ways faith has resulted in suffering, humiliation, and death. This contrasting picture of heroic faith begins with ἄλλοι δέ ("but others"), showing that some of the faithful did not experience victories like those listed in verses 32-35a. This contrast with verse 35a is strengthened by repeating the word "resurrection" in verse 35b, indicating that those who suffered looked forward to a "better resurrection" than the physical resurrection granted to people in verse 35a.[5]

This "better resurrection" brings into focus the important theme in Hebrews of the people of God looking forward to a future rest in the heavenly Jerusalem where citizenship is far more desirable than earthly citizenship (11:10, 13-16). The success stories of the faithful in verses 32-35a are inspiring, but in comparison to the "better resurrection" they pale in

---

[4]The precise meaning of τὸν ὀνειδισμὸν τοῦ Χριστοῦ is a matter of considerable debate. Moffatt, 180, says that "Moses encountered the same ὀνειδισμός" as Christ did afterwards; Windisch, 103, sees in v. 26 an interpretation of salvation history similar to 1 Cor 10:1ff. (the suffering of the people is a participation in the Messiah's sufferings); Montefiore, 203, calls τοῦ Χριστοῦ a reference to Ps 89(88):51-52, where the chosen people are called the "anointed"; Michel, 273-74, says τοῦ Χριστοῦ designates the Messiah (cf. 11:26 and 13:13) and any connection with Ps 88:51 is doubtful; Buchanan, 197, says the author of Hebrews "Assumed that Moses foresaw Messiah Jesus and acted accordingly. . . . [As all covenanters, he thought that] all prophecy applied only to the time of the Messiah"; and Spicq, 2:358, says the reproach is not an anticipation of the torments suffered by Christ, as in 10:33 and 13:13, but a concept similar to 2 Cor. 1:5; Phil 3:10; 1 Pet 4:13. The expectation of a heavenly city applied to the patriarchs in 11:10, 13-16 provides good evidence that the author believed that Moses saw Jesus through the eyes of faith and suffered for him, even as he saw his heavenly reward and lived for it.

[5]See Spicq, 2:369-71 for an excursus on "the better resurrection." Vanhoye, 191-92, states that 11:32-40 is designed to develop a great contrast between the two phases of faith, positive and negative. The hinge point, v. 35, is marked by ἄλλοι δέ and the opposition between the earthly resurrection (v. 35a) and the better resurrection (v. 35b).

significance. As Moses realized, according to 11:26, the reproach of Christ is worth far more than the treasures of Egypt.

In the other example lists there are numerous instances of antithesis, and some of the most effective are found in Isocrates, *To Philip* 60-61:

πεισθέντες γὰρ ὑπ' αὐτοῦ τῆς κατὰ θάλατταν δυνάμεως ἐπι-
θυμῆσαι καὶ τὴν κατὰ γῆν ἡγεμονίαν ἀπώλεσαν.

For because they were persuaded by him to covet the sovereignty of the sea, they lost even their leadership on land.[6]

τὴν ἀρχὴν αὐτοῖς γενέσθαι τῶν παρόντων κακῶν ὅτε τὴν ἀρχὴν τῆς θαλάττης ἐλάμβανον.

the rule of their present evils happened to them when the rule of the sea they seized.[7]

These antitheses, although well-crafted, actually are used to make points secondary to his main thesis of establishing a Panhellenic state. Such is not the case in *Archidamus* 42, 43, and 47, however, where Isocrates uses antitheses dramatically to argue his point on the possibility of the fewer conquering the more numerous. Each of his examples in this list has the same general sequence: the city or individual leader faced overwhelming odds, suffered dejection and wanted to give up; but a decision was made to fight, and as a result a great reversal in fortune occurred. Each story also has direct parallels with the present situation of Sparta and is therefore designed to incite patriotic fervor through showing how bravery led to unexpected reversals of fortune in the past. This theme of the great reversal is enhanced by antithesis:

ἐξ ὧν μὲν τοῖς ἄλλοις προσέταττον πρὸς τοὺς Ἕλληνας
    διαβληθέντας
ἐξ ὧν δὲ τοὺς ὑβρίζοντας ἠμύναντο παρὰ πᾶσιν ἀνθρώποις
    εὐδοκιμήσαντας.

as a result of dictating to others they lost repute with the Hellenes, while by defending themselves against insolent invaders they won fame among all mankind. (42)[8]

---

[6]*Isocrates*, vol. 1, trans. G. Norlin, LCL (New York: G. P. Putnam's Sons, 1928) 283.

[7]Since the Loeb translation does not adequately show this contrast, I have provided a more literal translation.

[8]*Isocrates*, 1.371.

ὥστε ὀλίγας ἡμέρας στερηθέντες τῶν αὐτῶν
   πολὺν χρόνον τῶν ἄλλων δεσπόται κατέστησαν.
after being deprived of their own possessions for but a few days, they became for many years masters of the rest of the world. (43)[9]

ἐπὶ μὲν τοῖς γεγενημένοις ἂν λυπηθεῖμεν
περὶ δὲ τῶν μελλόντων βελτίους ἐλπίδας ἂν λάβοιμεν.
over those things happening in the past we should be grieved;
concerning those things which are about to happen,
      we should be hopeful. (47).[10]

Similarly, in *Antidosis* 235 Isocrates uses antithesis to argue that rhetorical training does not corrupt people.

ὥστε Σόλων μὲν τῶν ἑπτὰ σοφιστῶν ἐκλήθη
καὶ ταύτην ἔσχε τὴν ἐπωνυμίαν τὴν νῦν ἀτιμαζομένην
   καὶ κρινομένην παρ' ὑμῖν.
Solon was named one of the seven sophists and was given the title which
is now dishonored and on trial here. (235)[11]

M. Aurelius III.3.1 employs ironic contrasts in illustrating the main
point of his list, the inevitability of death:

Hippocrates, after healing many a sick man, fell sick himself and died.
Many a death have Chaldeans foretold, and then their own fate has over-
taken them also. . . . Heraclitus, after endless speculations on the destruction of the world by fire, came to be filled internally with water, and died
beplastered with cowdung.[12]

Finally, in the Jewish document of 1 Maccabees 2:63 there is an ironic
contrast when Mattathias points out the difference between the lasting glory
received by those who are loyal to Torah and the short-lived glory of the
sinner whose ultimate destiny is destruction, saying of the sinner, "Today
he will be exalted, but tomorrow he will not be found."

---

[9]Ibid.

[10]As in *To Philip* 61 (see n. 7), I have provided a more literal translation.

[11]*Isocrates*, 2.317. Cf. *Antidosis* 233, an antithesis not designed to enhance the credibility of his main argument about rhetoricians.

[12]*The Communings with Himself of Marcus Aurelius Antoninus*, trans. C. R. Haines,
LCL (New York: G. P. Putnam's Sons, 1916) 49.

As with some of the contrasts in Hebrews 11, most of the contrasts in the example lists are not as tightly formulated or as pungently stated as the examples listed above. Indeed, it is questionable whether or not they should be classified as rhetorical antitheses. For example, the entire list in Aristotle, *Rhet.* II.23.11 is composed of a series of contrasts designed to prove that talented people are honored in spite of factors that normally dictate against such notariety.

> The Parians honoured Archilochus, in spite of his evil speaking; the Chians Homer, although he had rendered no public services; the Mytilenaeans Sappho, although she was a woman.[13]

Cicero's *De Oratore* III.136 is an editorial comment contrasting the wide-ranging knowledge of past orators with the narrow studies of present-day rhetoricians. The contrast is developed, however, through a longer explanation instead of a brief juxtaposition of clauses or particular words. Likewise, Plutarch's *On Love* 753D-F contrasts the lowly beginnings of certain poor or slave women with the powerful positions they attained through manipulation of great men. And in *On Love* 760C, the passive acceptance of the crude behavior of tyrants by three men is contrasted with the fierce opposition given by these three when tyrants made advances toward their boy lovers. A similar contrast is made in *On Love* 761C:

> It is a fact that men desert their fellow tribesmen and relatives and even (God knows) their parents and children; but lover and beloved, when their god is present, no enemy has ever encountered and forced his way through.[14]

Use of contrasts in the Jewish and Christian lists normally assumes this more lengthy type of formulation. Philo develops his thesis in *On the Virtues* 198-227 by contrasting the behavior of children with that of their parents, seeking to show that dishonorable children can arise from honorable parents and vice versa. The author of the Damascus Document contrasts good and bad behavior and illustrates the results of each (III.1-6, 10-16)

---

[13]*Rhetoric*, 307.

[14]Plutarch, *Moralia,* vol. 9, trans. W. C. Helmbold, LCL (Cambridge: Harvard University Press, 1927) 379.

in an attempt to show that God's destructive judgment results from following one's own desires, while divine reward follows faithfulness to the covenant. And 1 Clement 17-18 patterns its examples so that something great is said about each person in the list and then a contrasting statement is made about that person's humility. While lacking the rhetorical flare of the antitheses in Isocrates, these contrasts nevertheless can be quite persuasive in the development of their authors' viewpoints in their example lists.

Hyperbole, Paronomasia, and Circumlocution

Occasionally Hebrews 11 implements methods of exaggeration such as hyperbole to enhance a point. Quintilian defines hyperbole as "an elegant straining of the truth . . . employed . . . for exaggeration or attenuation" (VIII.6.67).[15] Its use may involve a metaphor (VIII.6.69),[16] and such metaphorical use of language may be seen in Hebrews 11:12b, where Abraham's advanced age is stressed by saying that his descendants were born of one who was "dead" (νενεκρωμένου, compare ἀποθανὼν ἔτι λαλεῖ in 11:4d).[17] Similarly, a simile from Genesis 22:17 is used in 11:12c-d where the great number of Abraham's descendants is stressed by saying that they are "as the stars in heaven in multitude and as the sand on the seashore in number."[18]

Hebrews 11 uses paronomasia more than hyperbole. As examined in detail in chapter 4, note 2, the use of sound to emphasize Sarah's barren condition (Σάρρα στεῖρα, 11:11a) has an effect something like saying "Sterile Cheryl" in English. Also noted above in chapter 3 is the repetition of "ōn" and "p" sounds and the word play on πίστις . . . ὑπόστασις in 11:1 that enhance the sound patterns in the definition of faith.

---

[15]*The Institutio Oratoria of Quintilian*, vol. 3, trans. H. E. Butler, LCL (Cambridge: Harvard University Press, 1921) 339. *Ad Her.* IV.44 calls it *superlatio*, an exaggeration for effect.

[16]Cf. *Ad Her.* IV.45; Arist., *Rhet.* III.2; *Poetics* 21; Cicero, *De Orator* 27.92; *De Oratore* III.38.155; and Dem. *On Style* 78.

[17]See also 12:1, where the saints of old are called a "cloud of witnesses."

[18]For simile, see *Ad Her.* IV.44; Arist. *Rhet.* III.11; Quint. VIII.3.72-81 and Dem. *On Style* 80.

Similarly, 11:33-34, 37 use *homoioptoton,* a paronomasia using similar case endings,[19] in conjunction with asyndeton to create a sense that the author is dealing with vast numbers of people. Homoioptoton also occurs in 11:5c-6b, where the repetition of the ending αι (μεμαρτύρηται εὐαρεστη-κέναι . . . εὐαρεστῆσαι πιστεῦσαι) combines with the repetition of εὐαρεστέω to help connect verse 6 to verse 5 and to strengthen the unity between faith and pleasing God. On the other hand, the sound repetition created by διέβησαν τὴν ἐρυθρὰν θάλασσαν in verse 29a,[20] and the word play on "God" in 11:16c (ὁ θεὸς θεός) seem designed simply to produce pleasing sounds.

Circumlocutions occur on several occasions in Hebrews 11 to express the identity of someone or someplace in the list. Hebrews 11:8 describes the land of Canaan, the "Promised Land" (verse 9a), as the "place which he [Abraham] was about to receive as an inheritance." This descriptive phrase helps to bring verses 7, 8, and 9 into a unity of thought, emphasizing the connection between faith and inheriting promises: τῆς κατὰ πίστιν δικαιοσύνης ἐγένετο κληρονόμος. . . . κληρονομίαν. . . . τῶν συγκληρονόμων τῆς ἐπαγγελίας. Similarly, the reference to God in 11:11b as the "One who promised" (τὸν ἐπαγγειλάμενον) stresses the aspect of God most important in this example, namely his faithfulness to do what he has promised. To help magnify the significance of Abraham's act of faith in sacrificing his "only son," verse 17b specifies Isaac (17a) as τὸν μονογενῆ, further illuminating the fact that Abraham was truly not looking at the matter in terms of physical possibilities.

According to Quintilian, one of the primary functions of circumlocution is verbal decoration.

> When we use a number of words to describe something for which one, or at any rate only a few words of description would suffice, it is called

---

[19]These can occur at the beginning, middle or end of a clause, and the words need not have the same number of syllables. See Quintilian IX.3.78-79 (491-93). Aristotle, *Rhet.* III.9.9 (393-95), calls it paromoiosis when there is similarity of the first or last syllables of clauses. *Ad Her.* IV.20.28 designates two or more words in the same case with the same endings (e.g., "Homin*em* laud*em* eqent*em* virtut*is,* abundant*em* felicitat*is?*"; cf. IV.22.31).

[20]Another instance may be in v. 28, where a number of "p" sounds occur.

periphrasis, that is, a circuitous mode of speech. It is sometimes necessary, being of special service when it conceals something which would be
indecent, if expressed in so many words. . . . But at times it is employed
solely for decorative effect, a practice most frequent among the poets. . . .
Still it is far from uncommon even in oratory, though in such cases it is
always used with greater restraint. For whatever might have been expressed with greater brevity, but is expanded for purposes of ornament, is
a *periphrasis,* to which we give the name *circumlocution.* (VIII.6.59-61)[21]

In the examples of circumlocution in Hebrews 11, however, more is at stake
than mere decoration. The descriptive phrases in 11:8a-b and 11a appear
to belong to a subset of circumlocution called *antonomasia* or *pronomi-*
natio, the replacing of a precise name with an epithet that describes physical attributes, character qualities, or external circumstances (*Ad Her.*
IV.42).

Quintilian states that antonomasia is commonly used by poets to indicate "the most striking characteristics of an individual, as in the phrase
describing Zeus as "Father of gods and king of men" (VIII.6.29).[22] Used
less frequently in oratory, an example of effective implementation is the
designation of Scipio as "the destroyer of Carthage and Numantia"
(VIII.6.30).[23] By comparison, note the way in which Hebrews 11:8 designates the "striking characteristic" of the Promised Land in this context
as the fact that it was given to Abraham as an "inheritance."

The descriptive phrase designating Isaac in 11:17b, in addition to being
antonomasia, functions in this case as an instance of *interpretatio.*

Interpretation is the figure which does not duplicate the same word by repeating it, but relaces the word that has been used by another of the same
meaning, as follows: "You have overturned the republic from its roots;
you have demolished the state from its foundations." . . . The hearer cannot but be impressed when the force of the first expression is renewed by
the explanatory synonym. (*Ad Her.* IV.28.38.)[24]

---

[21]*Quintilian,* 3.335, 337; cf. *Ad Her.* IV.33.

[22]*Quintilian,* 3.317, referring to *Aeneid* i. 65.

[23]Ibid., 319.

[24]*Rhetorica ad Herennium* 325. Cf. Quint. IX.3.98, who does not believe that it should
qualify to be called a figure of speech.

Although there is no attempt in Hebrews 11 to employ *interpretatio* in the rhetorical manner listed above (isocolon), the use of καὶ τὸν μονογενῆ in verse 17b definitely adds to the impact of the example: "By faith Abraham offered up Isaac, being tempted, *even his only son* he offered up, . . . unto whom it was said 'In Isaac shall your seed be called.' "[25]

There are other examples of synonymous terms in Hebrews 11. For example, verse 16a says the patriarchs desired something better, which verse 16b specifies as the heavenly (fatherland), and which verse 16d further defines as the city prepared for them by God. A similar instance of using synonymous phrases to strengthen an example occurs in verse 9. Stating that Abraham dwelt in the promised land as a "foreigner" (verse 9a), verse 9b clarifies this expression by saying that he dwelt in tents with Isaac and Jacob. Verse 9c then describes Abraham's sons as fellow heirs of the promise given to him by God (verse 9a). In other places in the list stylistic variations are apparently used simply to avoid repetition of the same term: ἀποθνῄσκων . . . τελευτῶν (11:21a, 22a); βασιλέως . . . Φαραώ (11:23c-24a); and ἄλλοι δέ . . . ἕτεροι δέ (11:35b, 36a).

Although none of these rhetorical devices is of major significance in itself, each enhances and strengthens the more important techniques in the example list. Through implementation of hyperbole, paronomasia, and circumlocution (especially *antonomasia, interpretatio* and *synonomy*), the rhetorical impact of the list in communicating the central importance of faith in the lives of those who please God is more firmly established.

---

[25]Cf. Heb 11:4b-c.

Chapter 7

Rhetorical Composition and Function of Hebrews 11

Function of Hebrews 11 in Its Total Context

Immediately prior to chapter 11, the author of Hebrews speaks to his audience in the language of exhortation. He commands and encourages through use of first-person plural subjunctives ("Let us come with a true heart in full assurance of faith . . . " [10:22]; "Let us hold fast the confession of hope without wavering" [10:23]) and second-person plural imperatives ("Remember the former days in which . . . you endured suffering . . . " [10:23]; "do not throw away your confidence, which has great reward . . . " [10:35]). In this way the author seeks to motivate his hearers to adopt or maintain his own tenacious commitment to belief in Christ and in the future reward promised by God.

Beginning with Hebrews 11:1, however, the language of exhortation ceases. With the exception of verse 3 the author speaks descriptively of events and concepts until 11:40, where he makes the transition back to addressing his audience directly with his concluding remark: "apart from us they will not be made perfect." In 12:1-13 he again exhorts and commands by using first-person plural subjunctives and second-person plural imperatives. So similar is the language in 12:1-13 to that of 10:19-39 that, if the mention of the great cloud of witnesses in 12:1 were omitted, all of Hebrews 11 could be left out and the sermon would proceed quite smoothly.

Nevertheless, the author carefully integrated Hebrews 11 into his sermon, and this appeal to salvation history has a definite function in his message. Observing this prompted Moffatt to write that the argument of 11:1-40 "flows directly out of $10^{35\text{-}39}$."[1] Windisch calls Hebrews 11 an insertion prompted by the citation in 10:38, and he compares its function to that of 4 Maccabees: calling on the audience to persevere through suffering by attempting to set aflame their courage through reciting a long series of former heirs of salvation.[2] Michel observes that Hebrews 10:19-39 prepares for the exposition of faith in Hebrews 11 by pointing to "faith" as the fundamental condition of salvation (10:22, 38, 39),[3] and Buchanan explains:

> From the standpoint of the exhortation in chapter ten, chapter eleven seems to be something of an intrusion, which could easily have been omitted and have the exhortation of 12:1 continue immediately after 10:39, but the author regularly related his doctrine to his homiletics, and his conclusion of chapter ten contained catchwords preparing the reader also for chapter eleven. Furthermore, chapter eleven is closely related to the introduction of the entire document, and it is consistent with the theology expressed throughout. If it was originally composed separately it has been well integrated into its present position.[4]

Buchanan is correct. Hebrews 11 plays a vital role in the author's overall attempt to instill in his discouraged audience a tenacious faith that will triumphantly face the present difficult circumstances.

The author repeatedly stresses the need to lead a life of hope focused on the heavenly reward that awaits the faithful when they exit from this world.[5] Jesus' death has inaugurated a new covenant vastly superior to the old Mosaic covenant,[6] and in light of this momentous sacrificial death of

---

[1]Moffatt, 158.

[2]Windisch, 98.

[3]Michel, 368-69.

[4]Buchanan, 104.

[5]See, e.g., the use of ἐλπίς in 3:6; 6:11, 18; 7:19; 10:23. Cf. 11:10, 16; 12:22; 13:14 on the heavenly city, and 2:1-4; 3:6-4:13; 6:1-12; 10:19-39; 12:25-29 on the dangers of falling away from the faith. Cf. H. Braun, "Das himmlische Vaterland bei Philo und im Hebräerbrief," in *Verborum Veritas,* Festschrift für G. Stahlin, ed. O. Böcher and K. Haacker (Wuppertal: Brockhaus, 1970).

[6]E.g., 1:1-14; 7:11–10:18.

the Son of God, no notion of turning away from the Christian confession can be tolerated.[7] Since the author knows that some of those to whom he writes are considering precisely such an action (2:1-4; 3:7-4:13; 5:11-6:12; 10:25-31), he repeatedly addresses this problem both directly and indirectly in his sermon.

After constructing an exalted portrait of Jesus in chapter 1, the author warns in 2:1-4,

> In light of this it is extremely necessary for us to heed what we have heard, *lest we fall away*. For if the word that was spoken by angels was firmly established and every transgression and disobedience received its deserved retribution, *how shall we escape if we neglect such a great salvation* which was confirmed unto us by those who heard it proclaimed at first by the Lord, [and which was] testified at the same time by God with signs and wonders and various miracles, and the Holy Spirit [making] distributions according to his will?

Again stressing the stability of faith in 3:6b, the author says that he and his audience are the house of God over which Jesus has been placed "*if* we hold firm the boldness and the boast of hope."[8]

Showing with an Old Testament proof text how the Israelites failed to enter God's promised rest because they hardened their hearts (3:7-11), he pointedly delivers his message:

> Watch out, brothers, lest there be in anyone of you *an evil heart of unbelief causing you to fall away from the living God*. But encourage each other every day . . . so that none of you might be hardened by the deception of sin, for we have become partakers of Christ *if we hold firm our confidence until the end*. (3:12-13)

Warning that the disobedient Israelites failed to enter God's rest because of their disbelief (3:15-18), he exhorts his listeners, "Therefore let us fear lest, leaving behind the promise, anyone from you falls short of entering God's rest" (4:1). He reveals his concern over potential apostasy when he then draws strong parallels with the disobedient Israelites:

---

[7]Heb. 3:7-15; 6:4-8; 10:26-31.

[8]ℵ, A, C, D, Ψ, 0121b, 𝔐, lat, and syr^p all add "until the end," which, if not original, is certainly in keeping with the rest of Hebrews. See 3:14; 6:11.

> For we also heard the good news just as they did, but the word they heard did not benefit them because it was not combined with faith (πίστις) in those who heard. For we who believe (πιστεύσαντες) enter the rest. . . . Therefore let us make haste to enter that rest, so that no one might fall into the same pattern of disobedience. (4:2-3, 11)

Concern over their spiritual condition comes through strongly in 5:11-14, where he accuses them of being spiritual babies although they have had sufficient time to become teachers. Warning that restoration of those committing apostasy is impossible (6:4-8), he adds in 6:9-10 that he does not expect this to happen to them. The author deeply desires his audience to develop a bold and tenacious faith, and he reiterates his theme of endurance in 6:11-12: "And we desire each of you to *demonstrate the same zeal unto the full assurance of hope until the end,* so that you will not be sluggish but imitators of those who *through faith and patience inherit the promises. "*

The author's concern for the wavering faith of his hearers again reveals itself in the exhortation of 10:23: "Let us hold firm the confession of hope without wavering, for the One who promised is faithful." Noting that some have already withdrawn from the Christian assembly (10:25), he stresses in 10:26-31 that terrible judgment awaits those who commit the sin of apostasy. But the author desires to encourage his listeners as well as to threaten, so he assures them in 10:32-39 that he expects a better future for them (cf. 6:9-10). Yet even in the midst of this assurance he warns, "Therefore do not cast away your boldness (or confidence), which has great reward. For you have need of patience so that, doing the will of God, you might receive the promise" (10:35-36).

Similarly, after the example list in Hebrews 11, the author writes, "With patience let us run the race set before us. . . . Consider the one who endured from sinners hostility against himself so that you do not become weary in your souls, losing courage" (12:1, 3). And in 12:12-13, 16-17 he exhorts them to lift their drooping hands and straighten their weak knees, taking care not to miss the grace of God like Esau, who, after selling his birthright, could not repent even though he tried. Seeing the danger of falling away to be very real for these people, the author strives to convince them to remain faithful through a variety of means: Old Testament proof texts, expositions, explanations, warnings, and exhortations. His use of the example list in Hebrews 11 is one more dimension of this effort, for here he seeks to demonstrate that faith in God's promises has from the beginning of time involved endurance.

The exhortation of Hebrews 10:19-39 prepares the listeners for the example list. According to 10:35-36, God's promised salvation is a reward for faithfulness, and 10:23 indicates that Christians can confidently and boldly maintain their confession of hope. Any reproaches they have suffered (ὀνειδισμοῖς, 10:33) are insignificant compared to the "better and lasting possessions" awaiting them in heaven (κρείττονα ὕπαρξιν καὶ μένουσαν, 10:34). (Compare κρείττονος ὀρέγονται τοῦτ᾽ ἔστιν ἐπουρανίου in 11:16 ["they desire a better (homeland), that is the heavenly one"] and τὴν τοὺς θεμελίους ἔχουσαν πόλιν ἧς τεχνίτης καὶ δημιουργὸς ὁ θεός in 11:10 ["the city having foundations, whose builder and maker is God"] and in 11:26 Moses' belief that the ὀνειδισμός of Christ is worth more than the treasures of Egypt).

After exhorting his audience to faith in 10:19-38 and affirming the existence of their faith in 10:39, in Hebrews 11 the author provides an extended series of examples to illustrate the characteristics of faith that please God. The faith demanded in 10:19-39 is the faith described in 11:1-38; and following the conclusion to the list in 11:39-40, exhortation is mixed with illustration in 12:1-13 as the author appeals to the example of Jesus as a model of heroic faith to emulate (12:2-3). The exhortations to faithfulness are strongly motivational, as is the concrete evidence from salvation history that men and women of faith lived heroically in spite of adversity.

These heroes of the past tenaciously held to their belief in the truth of God's promise of heavenly reward, even though they had far less evidence of its reality than the Christians addressed in this homily. This provides tangible evidence that such a life of faith is possible. The example list demonstrates that from the dawn of time faith has involved turning away from the world, viewing heavenly realities as more important than worldly. If those who hear this sermon desire to join the society of God's faithful in the promised heavenly city, they must follow the example of this great cloud of witnesses.

Rhetorical Study of Hebrews 11

Since the author of Hebrews consciously implemented artistic use of language in his efforts at persuasion, failure to recognize these rhetorical techniques is failure to appreciate fully the impact of his words. The force of his message diminishes when one does not hear the oral artistry represented by the symbols printed on the page of a book. He wrote his sermon to impact the *ears* of his audience, to *sound* persuasive. Consequently, listening to the Greek text opens up new horizons of understanding and appreciation of the work.

Hebrews 11 obviously communicates the need to remain faithful, but studying the rhetorical composition of this example list reveals how intensely the author pursued this goal. Furthermore, comparing Hebrews 11 with other ancient example lists underscores another fact. The rhetorical techniques employed in this great chapter on faith primarily enhance the impression that the exemplary people listed are representative of a multitude of others who could also be cited as evidence. The author does not merely marshall an impressive array of evidential material; he makes this evidence appear to represent a timeless statement of truth presented in 11:1.

Yet even the definition of faith in verse 1 reveals more than a precise statement on the nature of faith. Concentrated attention on the sounds produced by its two brief clauses shows that the author was concerned to produce more than just a philosophically correct formulation of words. He wanted the descriptive clauses to sound persuasive, and this concern probably played as much a role in the selection of ὑπόστασις as did the philosophical history of the term. His goal was to motivate his audience to action, and the meaning of faith is made abundantly clear by the larger context in which the definition is located.

The driving rhythm of verses 3-31, constantly reinforcing that faith motivated the actions of the heroes listed, is an oral technique. One need only recall the "I have a dream" speech delivered by Martin Luther King, Jr. to realize the potential power of this kind of rhetoric. King creates a kind of anticipation in his oration. The audience begins to feel the arrival of the next advent of that powerful phrase: "I have a dream." Repetition reinforced the message and gave greatly increased impact to the truth of his words. So it is with Hebrews 11:3-31. The author intensifies motivation as he parades each hero of faith before his audience, revealing how they remained true and finally conquered over worldly opposition.

What scholars have not previously noted, however, is that the intensity of the author's rhetoric does not diminish after 11:31. The power of the anaphoric πίστει is continued by different means in 11:32-40. The goal remains the same; the method changes. And study of these verses in light of the ancient rhetorical handbooks brings to light the significance of this section.

Scholars have observed the rhetorical interruption at 11:32 but have failed to see the full significance of the oratorical techniques that follow. What the author states explicitly in 11:32—that continued recounting of exemplary people is possible but too time consuming—he implies by the use of asyndeton, isocolon, and chiasm in the ensuing verses. Simply stating that there are more examples is not enough. He proceeds to give impressions of faithfulness that bring the era of fearless belief in God up to the present time. The author does not want his audience to think that such actions are merely a thing of the past, so he constructs his brief statements on heroes of faith to make them appear to represent a universal principle.

In conclusion, studying the rhetorical structure of Hebrews 11 brings new insight into the method employed by an ancient missionary at work trying to exhort a discouraged group of Christians. Quietly reading his words in the privacy of one's individual study in some ways inhibits feeling their force. The contemporary norm of silent reading, especially speed reading, works against a sympathetic hearing of the words. One should take the time to listen to the Greek words as if an ancient oral culture, recognizing that the author of Hebrews considered the success of his message to be largely dependent on the way it sounded to his audience. As he preaches to them, his many efforts at oral artistry in the construction of his utterances are not peripheral but central to his purpose. To experience this is to add a new dimension to understanding and responding to his words.

Use of *Exempla*
according to the Rhetorical Handbooks

Introduction

The frequent use of *exempla* in the literature of antiquity witnesses to the perceived effectiveness of this rhetorical technique. There is evidence of collections of *exempla* that served as resource books for rhetoricians. Bennett J. Price calls attention to the report of Diogenes Laertius (v.80-81) that Demetrius of Phaleron (ca. 350-280 B.C.E.) produced a collection of Aesop's fables; and he observes that despite Pseudo-Aristotle's claim in the introduction to *Oeconomica* II.1.8 (1345a 25-31) that the purpose of the document was not to provide examples for orators, Book II is nevertheless an extensive list of anecdotes compiled on the topic of how various peoples and heads of state raised revenue.[1] Commenting on the great value placed upon exemplary figures in the Greco-Roman world, Price observes that Cornelius Nepos compiled at least five books of examples, Hyginus gathered *exempla,* Valerius Maximus produced nine or ten books of his *Facta et Dicta Memorabilia,* which were arranged in thematic categories, and the "first books of Livy can almost be considered a chronologically arranged *exempla* collection."[2] The existence of books of examples de-

---

[1] "'Paradeigma' and 'Exemplum' in Ancient Rhetorical Theory" (Ph.D. diss., University of California at Berkeley, 1975) 85.

[2] Ibid., 86-87 (citing *Aul. Gell.* VI.18.11; X.18.7). See also 177-79 and n. 66 on 290-92 for information on *exempla* collections in Quintilian.

signed to be used by orators as reference works reveals a tendency toward adoption of standard *exempla* which were employed widely to prove or illustrate points. This tendency to recycle examples is also evident in ancient rhetorical handbooks, where some of the same examples are used by the various authors to illustrate specific rhetorical techniques.[3] In these handbooks, from Aristotle through Quintilian, there are also important explanations of the purpose, content, and function of *exempla*.

A. Aristotle's *Rhetoric*

Aristotle understands rhetoric as the attempt "to discover the real and apparent means of persuasion" (I.1.14),[4] and his philosophical approach may be seen in the way he classifies examples and explains where and how they can be used most effectively. He defines three categories of speeches: (1) the deliberative, which is used by statesmen to recommend one course of action as better than another in matters of war and peace, the defense of the country, imports and exports, legislation, and so forth (I.3.5; 4.7); (2) the forensic, which is employed in law courts to determine what is just and unjust (I.3.5); and (3) the epideictic, whose goal (τέλος) is to reveal what is honorable and dishonorable (I.3.5). "Examples [παραδείγματα] are most suitable for deliberative speakers," says Aristotle, "for it is by examination of the past that we divine and judge the future" (I.9.40).[5]

Aristotle specifies two different kinds of examples: things that actually happened (πράγματα προγεγενημένα), and stories one invents (τὸ αὐτὸν ποιεῖν), which he further divides into comparison (παραβολή) and fable (λόγος) (II.20.2). He illustrates παραβολή by quoting a pointed remark from Socrates: "magistrates should not be chosen by lot, for this would be the same as choosing as representative athletes not those competent to contend, but those on whom the lot falls" (II.20.4).[6] Aristotle defines λόγοι as tales such as those told by Aesop which illustrate their

---

[3]The author of *Rhet. ad Her.* IV.1.1-6.9 argues against the use of standardized examples.

[4]*Rhetoric,* trans. John H. Freese, LCL (New York: G. P. Putnam's Sons, 1926) 13.

[5]Ibid., 105.

[6]Ibid., 275.

points by analogy, through the telling of stories about animals discussing things, and so forth (II.20.5-8). He does not comment, however, on the use of stories from Homer or the other poets whose writings were considered sacred by the majority of the Greeks.

Aristotle asserts that the most convincing form of argumentation for the orator is the enthymeme, because it proceeds deductively from a universal to a particular. To argue inductively by basing one's argument on examples is an inferior method which lacks the cogency of the deductive approach. "Now arguments that depend on examples are not less calculated to persuade, but those which depend upon enthymemes meet with greater approval" (I.2.10).[7] Inductive argumentation may be attacked because it lacks a universal:

> It is neither the relation of part to whole, nor of whole to part, nor of one whole to another whole, but of part to part, of like to like, when both come under the same genus, but one of them is better known than the other. (I.2.19)[8]

Ideally, therefore, examples should come toward the end, functioning as witnesses to the truth of the argument, rather than at the beginning, functioning as proofs.

> If we have no enthymemes, we must employ examples as demonstrative proofs [ἀποδείξεσιν], for conviction [πίστις] is produced by these;

---

[7]Ibid., 21.

[8]Ibid., 29. Cf. *Prior Analytics,* where he says:

Thus it is evident that an example (παράδειγμα) represents the relation, not of part to whole or of whole to part, but of one part to another, where both are subordinate to the same general term, and one of them is known. It differs from induction in that the latter, as we saw, shows from an examination of all the individual cases that the [major] extreme applies to the middle, and does not connect the conclusion with the [minor] extreme; whereas the example does connect it and does use all the individual cases for its proof (II.24, trans. Hugh Tredennick, LCL [Cambridge: Harvard University Press, 1938] 517).

In *Problems* 18.3 Aristotle says, "We more readily believe in facts to which many bear witness, and examples and tales are like witnesses; furthermore, belief through witnesses is easy."

but if we have them, examples must be used as evidence and as a kind of epilogue to the enthymemes. For if they stand first, they resemble induction, and induction is not suitable to rhetorical speeches except in very few cases; if they stand last they resemble evidence, and a witness is in every case likely to induce belief. Wherefore also it is necessary to quote a number of examples if they are put first, but one alone is sufficient if they are put last; for even a single trustworthy witness is of use. (II.20.9)[9]

Almost by definition, therefore, an example list would be considered part of an inferior means of proving a point or an unnecessary multiplication of witnesses to a deductively proven argument. He does concede, however, that the ideal of a deductive proof is not always possible; and in such cases he would recognize the use of a series of examples to prove one's case. Nevertheless, there is no discussion in Aristotle's *Rhetoric* of the use of example lists.

B. *Rhetorica ad Alexandrum*

Rhetorica ad Alexandrum, a treatise preserved among the works of Aristotle but probably written by an anonymous author of a sophistic school around the beginning of the third century B.C.E. as a handbook for orators,[10] has only a small amount of information on the use of *exempla*. The author does not preserve Aristotle's division of examples into historical events and fabricated stories. He describes only the historical example and does not mention παραβολή and λόγος.

Examples [παραδείγματα] are actions that have occurred previously and are similar to, or the opposite of, those which we are now discussing. They should be employed on occasions when your statement of the case is unconvincing [ἄπιστον] and you desire to illustrate it, if it cannot be proved by the argument from probability, in order that your audience may be more ready to believe your statements when they realize that another action resembling the one you allege has been committed in the way in which you say that it occurred.

---

[9]*Rhetoric*, 279.

[10]See *Rhetorica ad Alexandrum*, trans. H. Rackman, LCL (Cambridge: Harvard University Press, 1937) 250-61. Quintilian III.4.9 attributes the work to Anaximenes.

> There are two modes of examples. This is because some things happen according to reasonable expectation, others against reasonable expectation. . . . (1429a 21-29)[11]

Thus, the division made by the author is between historical examples used as comparisons and as contrasts. In his view, such examples are persuasive because of their similarity to or difference from the present event under consideration. But although he does not retain Aristotle's categories, he agrees that the primary function of the example is an alternative to deductive argumentation.

He goes on to explain how to use examples both when arguing for what one's audience would naturally expect to be true and when going against the expectations of one's audience. As an example of an argument which is designed to go against normal reasoning, he gives an example list consisting primarily of Greek nations instead of individual people.

> . . . if one wanted to prove that numbers are not the cause of victory, one would use as examples events that have happened contrary to probability: one would tell how the exiles at Athens with fifty men to start with captured Phyle and fought the far more numerous party in the city with their Spartan allies, and so got back to their own city; and how the Thebans, when Boeotia was invaded by the Spartans and almost the whole of the Peloponnesians, took the field at Leuctra single-handed and defeated the Spartan forces; and how the Syracusan Dion with 3,000 heavy infantry sailed to Syracuse and waged a victorious war against Dionysius who had a force many times as large; and similarly how the Corinthians coming to the aid of the Syracusans with nine triremes defeated the Carthaginians in spite of the fact that they were blockading the harbors of Syracuse with 150 vessels and held the whole of the city except the citadel. To sum up, these and similar instances of actions accomplished against reasonable expectation usually succeed in discrediting counsels of policy that are based on probability. Such is the nature of examples. (1429b 6-25)[12]

Agreeing with Aristotle that examples should come after one's proofs, the author of *Ad Alexandrum* also comments on their proper use, "We must

---

[11]Ibid., 327.

[12]Ibid., 329.

take examples that are akin to the case and those that are nearest in time or place to our hearers, and if such are not available, such others as are most important and best known'' (1439a 1-3).[13] He deems it important for the listeners to be acquainted with the stories in order for the example to have optimum effect. But in spite of the fact that an audience could be very familiar with the mythological stories from Homer, the author makes no mention of using such stories as examples. Ideally, *exempla* persuasively recount well-known events from recent history to *illustrate* the validity of a case that is otherwise unconvincing.

C. Rhetorica ad Herennium

Rhetorica ad Herennium was apparently written around 80 B.C.E., and whether or not the author was a certain Cornificius or an anonymous orator is of no particular concern here.[14] Although written several centuries after *Ad Alexandrum, Ad Herennium* is the earliest extant Latin rhetorical handbook. The author benefits a great deal from the earlier Greek rhetoricians, but he pointedly disagrees with the dominant viewpoint of his contemporary Greek orators on the issue of the *exemplum*. Apparently, as the use of examples in oratory developed over the years, there came to be widespread beliefs about their proper use. One of these was that, since examples function as witnesses to the truth (cf. Aristotle, *Rhetoric* II.20.9 and *Ad Alex.* 1429a 21-29), they should come from eminently respected sources, namely famous orators of the past. This becomes clear at the beginning of *Ad Herennium* IV where the author finds it necessary to defend his own practice of inventing examples when illustrating particular points. Concerning the attitude of current Greek teachers of rhetoric, he says,

> after they have given their own precepts on how to embellish style, they must for each kind of embellishment offer an example drawn from a reputable orator or poet. And their first ground is that in doing so they are

---

[13]Ibid., 393.

[14]Price, ''Paradeigma,'' 88, says that Cornificius was the author, while Harry Caplan, trans. *Rhetorica ad Herennium,* LCL (Cambridge: Harvard University Press, 1954) vii, ix-xiv, argues that Cornificius lived considerably later than the era in which the book was written.

prompted by modesty, because it seems a kind of ostentation not to be content [with] . . . an example from Ennius, or . . . from Gracchus. . . .

In the second place, examples, they say, serve the purpose of testimony; for, like the testimony of a witness, the example reinforces what the precept has suggested and only to a slight degree effected. . . . an example is used just like testimony to prove a point; it should properly therefore be taken only from a writer of highest reputation, lest what ought to serve as proof of something else should itself require proof. . . . does not the very prestige of the ancients not only lend greater authority to their doctrine but also sharpen in men the desire to imitate them? Yes, it excites the ambitions and whets the zeal of all men when the hope is implanted in them of being able by imitation to attain to the skill of a Gracchus or a Crassus. (IV.1.1-2.2)[15]

The author is not convinced by such claims for modesty or the surpassing worth of past *exempla*. Confidently he asserts, ''We need not yield to antiquity in everything'' (IV.2.4). Spurning modesty that is timid to invent *exempla*, he proves his point with what Aristotle would call παραβολή (one of the subcategories of παράδειγμα)[16] but what this author calls *similitudo*, not *exemplum*.[17]

It is as if some one should come to the Olympic games to run, and having taken a position for the start, should accuse of impudence those who have begun the race—should himself stand within the barrier and recount to others how Ladas used to run, or Boiscus in the Isthmian games. These Greek rhetoricians do likewise. (IV.3.4)[18]

The author goes on to say that it takes no great skill to select examples from others but it does to create one's own. In his opinion an example should be proof of the speaker's own skill (IV.4.7-6.9).

According to *Ad Herennium, exempla* should never function as proofs but merely as illustrations, regardless of whether they come from an ancient or a modern speaker. Disagreeing with his Greek contemporaries who

---

[15]*Ad Herennium,* 229-33.

[16]*Rhetoric* II.20.2-4.

[17]*Ad Her.* IV.45.59-48.61.

[18]Ibid., 235.

say, "Since examples correspond to testimony, it is proper that, like testimony, they should be taken from men of the highest reputation," he responds,

> First and foremost, examples are set forth, not to confirm or bear witness, but to clarify [Primum omnium, exempla ponuntur nec confirmandi neque testificandi causa, sed demonstrandi]. . . . The difference between testimony and example is this: by example we clarify the nature of our statement, while by testimony we establish its truth. (IV.3.5)[19]

In making this assertion, he relegates examples to a slightly lower position of importance than does Aristotle, for he does not say that they can be used to prove a point but only to clarify it. In *Rhetoric* II.20.9 Aristotle merely says that they are a less desirable form of proof than the use of an enthymeme.

In spite of what the author asserts to be the proper function of *exempla,* however, within *Ad Herennium* itself his use of examples does not always conform to his own stated viewpoint. In IV.49.62 he says theoretically,

> Exemplification [exemplum] is the citing of something done or said in the past, along with the definite naming of the doer or author. It is used with the same motives as a Comparison [similitudo]. It renders a thought more brilliant when used for no other purpose than beauty; clearer, when throwing more light upon what was somewhat obscure; more plausible, when giving the thought greater verisimilitude; more vivid, when expressing everything so lucidly that the matter can, I may almost say, be touched by the hand.[20]

Yet, although he classifies *exempla* as embellishments to the speech which are to follow one's proofs (see II.18.28, 29.46),[21] he sometimes employs examples other than in this way. Price observes that in II.19.29 *exempla*

---

[19]Ibid., 237-39.

[20]Ibid., 383-85.

[21]" . . . embellishment consists of similes, examples, amplifications, previous judgments, and the other means which serve to expand and enrich the argument" (*Ad Herennium* II.29.46; LCL, 141). This order of placing *exempla* after the proof is similar to that presented in Aristotle's *Rhet.* II.20.9.

are used to strengthen the proof by argument from analogy rather than merely to adorn it.[22]

D. Cicero

Cicero's works on rhetoric span a time period of forty years. Addressed to different individuals and written for different reasons, these books present no one consistent view of *exempla*. The only consistent factor is Cicero's understanding that examples are designed to persuade the audience by affecting their emotions, not their intellect.[23] In *De Inventione*, a youthful work of Cicero which was later somewhat of an embarrassment to him,[24] he places *exemplum* in a subcategory under comparison.

> . . . probability which depends on *comparison* [*comparabile*] involves a certain principle of similarity running through diverse material. It has three subdivisions, similitude [*imago*], parallel [*collatio*], example [*exemplum*]. A *similitude* is a passage setting forth a likeness of individuals or characters. A *parallel* is a passage putting one thing beside another on the basis of their resemblances. An *example* supports or weakens a case by appeal to precedent or experience, citing some person or historical event. (I.30.49)[25]

In *Topica* 10.41-45 Cicero presents material similar to that just cited from *De Inventione*, placing *exemplum* in a subcategory of *similitudo*.

> Under the same topic of similarity comes also the citing of examples or parallel cases, as Crassus in his defence of Curius cited many cases of men who, having been named as heirs in the event that a son was born within ten months and died before attaining his majority, would have taken the inheritance. Such a citation of parallel cases carried the day, and you jurists make frequent us of it in your responses [eaque vos in respondendo uti multum soletis]. (10.44)[26]

---

[22]Price, "Paradeigma," 90.

[23]Ibid., 127.

[24]See *De Oratore* I.5.

[25]Cicero, *De Inventione,* trans. H. M. Hubbell, LCL (Cambridge: Harvard University Press, 1949) 89, 91.

[26]Cicero, *Topica,* trans. H. M. Hubbell, LCL (Cambridge: Harvard University Press, 1949) 415.

This recognition of the importance of examples in arguing one's case surpasses that seen in the previous rhetorical handbooks. Cicero even adds that fictitious examples of similarity [ficta exempla similitudinis] are valuable in oratory when used hyperbolically as comparisons, though usually these are not employed in judicial cases (10.45).[27] His appreciation for the effectiveness of *exempla* seems far greater than that of *Ad Her.* IV.49.62, which relegates them to embellishments of a speech. In his works on rhetoric, however, Cicero actually says very little about *exempla*.[28] On a theorectical level he offers minimal explanation; but on a practical level it is obvious from reading his own speeches that he found the *exemplum* to be a very effective tool for argumentation, and he did not merely use it to illustrate points previously proven by deductive means.[29]

E. Quintilian

Writing during the ninth decade of the first century C.E., in *Institutio Oratoria* Quintilian provides a very complete explanation of his understanding of the use of *exempla*.

> The third kind of proof, which is drawn into the service of the case from without, is styled a παράδειγμα by the Greeks, who apply the term to all comparisons of like with like, but more especially to historical parallels. Roman writers have for the most part preferred to give the name of comparison [*similitudo*] to that which the Greeks style παραβολή, while they translate παράδειγμα by example [*exemplum*], although this latter involves comparison [*simile*], while the former is of the nature of an example [*exemplum*]. For my own part, I prefer with a view to making my purpose easier of apprehension to regard both as παραδείγματα and to call them examples [*exempla*]. Nor am I afraid of being thought to disa-

---

[27]Price, "Paradeigma," 111, believes that in this passage *exemplum* is a genus consisting of two species: *facta* and *ficta exempla*.

[28]See ibid., 103-29 for a detailed investigation of *exemplum* in Cicero's works.

[29]E.g., in his initial section of *In Catilinam,* at the very beginning of his speech Cicero employs two *exempla* in I.1.3. In *Pro Milone* 3.7 he uses an example in arguing from the greater to the lesser, and in *Pro Milone* 27.72 he uses another to argue from the lesser to the greater (cf. *Pro Milone* 4.9). In *Pro Murena* 8.17 he even uses an example from his own recent past to argue a point.

gree with Cicero, although he does separate comparison [*collatio*] from example [*exemplum*]. For he divides all arguments into two classes, induction and ratiocination [*inductionem et ratiocinationem*], just as most Greeks divide it into παραδείγματα and ἐπιχείρηματα, explaining παράδειγμα as rhetorical induction (ῥητορικὴν ἐπαγωγήν). (V.11.1-2)[30]

Thus, unlike *Ad Herennium*, Quintilian classifies *exemplum* as a legitimate aspect of inductive argumentation, not just as embellishment. He admits in V.11.5 that *similitudo* is sometimes used for embellishment but quickly adds, "at present I am concerned with the use of similitude in proof." His classification system agrees with Aristotle's, for he says that παράδειγμα/*exemplum* consists of παράδειγμα/*exemplum* (= historical example) and παραβολή/*similitudo*.

Quintilian asserts that the historical parallel is more commonly used than the simile when seeking to persuade an audience with *exempla,* and he calls the historical parallel the most important in this class of proofs from induction (V.11.6). Concerned that his readers should employ this inductive approach correctly, he adds, "We must therefore consider whether the parallel is complete or only partial, that we may know whether to use it in its entirety or merely to select those portions which are serviceable" (V.11.6).[31] Price argues that Quintilian is speaking here of written collections of *exempla* (that is, sourcebooks), asserting that "there is little hazard that a speaker who composes his own examples . . . will cite whole chapters of Livy when only one action of Livy's heroes is relevant."[32] Quintilian's advice is important in evaluating the effective construction of an example: The presupposed knowledge by an author's audience of the story used as an example determines whether it is most effective to quote the historical parallel in its entirety or merely to allude to it.[33]

---

[30]Quintilian, *Institutio Oratoria,* vol. II, trans. H. E. Butler, LCL (New York: G. P. Putnam's Sons, 1921) 271-73.

[31]Ibid., 275.

[32]"Paradeigma," 178. Note that in Chapters 2-3 Plutarch and Clement at times do not have a very good sense of how much of a story to tell.

Whereas the other rhetorical handbooks do not mention using documents considered sacred by most Greeks, particularly Homer's works, Quintilian states that one can sometimes enhance an argument by employing an *exemplum* from these sources:

> A similar method [that is, telling all or only part of a story] is to be pursued in quoting from the fictions of the poets [quae ex poeticis fabulis ducuntur], though we must remember that they will be of less force as proofs.[34]

He quotes *Pro Milone* 3.8 as an example of how Cicero effectively used fables from Hesiod and Aesop in arguing a case, and he refers to Menenius Agrippa's use of a fable to bring reconciliation between the plebs and patricians.[35] As Aristotle indicated in *Rhetoric* I.1.12, people who cannot follow logical proofs are often persuaded by the use of examples. Similarly, Quintilian says that Aesop's fables "are specially attractive to rude and uneducated minds, which are less suspicious than others in their reception of fictions [ficta] and, when pleased, readily agree with the arguments from which their pleasure is derived" (V.11.19).[36]

F. Conclusions

Rhetorical use of examples was considered effective enough to warrant their collection into resource books for orators, and descriptions of their proper use may be read in the ancient rhetorical handbooks. In spite of evolution of thought and minor differences in categorizing, the theoretical descriptions written from Aristotle through Quintilian have much in common on the function of *exempla*. Of all these handbooks, only *Ad Herennium* denies that examples may be used to prove one's point in a speech;

---

[33]As an example of giving an entire story, he cites Cicero's *Pro Milone* 4.9, and as an example of merely alluding to a well-known story he cites *Pro Milone* 3.8 (Quintilian, IV.11.15-16).

[34]Ibid., 281.

[35]See Livy II.32 for the story.

[36]Quintilian, *Institutio Oratoria,* 2:283. Quintilian gives further information about exempla in other places in his *Inst. Or.,* but the primary passages are in Book V.11.1-21. See Price, "Paradeigma," 131-210, for a detailed study.

and even the author of this book at times uses examples as part of proofs.[37] Aristotle maintains that inductive arguments involving *exempla* are not as persuasive as deductive proofs, and there appears to have been agreement on this point among the other rhetorical-handbook authors. Ideally one should employ examples as testimonies to the truth of something previously proven, but under some circumstances they can be very effective, particularly for convincing uneducated people. And although the rhetorical handbooks most often speak of the use of historical examples that are parallel to the case under consideration, one may also employ historical events that contrast with the case (*Ad Alex.* 1429a 21-29), forming an antithesis.

Aristotle and the author of *Ad Alexandrum* view examples as ideally playing a secondary role of illustrating or witnessing to the truth, whereas *Ad Her.* IV.49.62 classifies them as mere embellishment. Cicero and Quintilian show a softening of this viewpoint, expressing more optimism about the role played by examples in proving a case. Yet, in spite of the fact that Cicero states in *Topica* 10.44 that Crassus cited many examples of historical parallels in his defense of Curius, and that jurists frequently use such examples in their responses, he never mentions the use of example lists per se. None of the rhetorical handbooks comments on the composition and/or function of lists of famous people.

---

[37]Price, ''Paradeigma,'' 90-95.

Distinctions between Greco-Roman and Jewish and Christian Lists

There are several noticeable differences between Jewish and Christian lists on the one hand and Greco-Roman lists on the other. Jewish and Christian example lists tend to use well-known people either as *models* of good behavior to imitate or as bad behavior to avoid, placing considerable emphasis on moral virtues. 1 Maccabees 2:50-60 consists entirely of Old Testament men who were faithful to God; 4 Maccabees 18:10-19 lists only the actions or sayings of Old Testament worthies; and 4 Ezra 7:106-11 cites only Old Testament figures who prayed on behalf of others. Wisdom 10, aside from the first example on Cain's murder of Abel, only lists Old Testament figures who were guided by Wisdom. The author of Wisdom is so intent on portraying these Old Testament people in a positive light that he whitewashes Jacob in 10:10 and the Israelite people in 10:15-21, presenting their righteousness without any mention of their faults. Conversely, CD II.14–IV.2 consists primarily of examples of negative behavior, of people who disobeyed God and were punished as a result.

Although Philo's purpose in composing the list in *Quis Rerum* 260-62 is not to provide models for imitation, he does seek to demonstrate through his examples of Noah, Isaac, Jacob, and Moses that only the righteous receive prophetic inspiration from God. Likewise, in *De Virt.* 198-227 there is a strong affirmation of virtuous behavior in the list. 1 Clement 4-6 provides negative examples, showing how righteous people suffered ill effects due to the jealousy of others. Conversely, 1 Clement 9-12 and 17-18 consist entirely of positive examples from the Old Testament, and the purpose of 1 Clem 17-18 to provide models for good behavior is clearly stated in 17:1: Μιμηταὶ γενώμεθα . . . ("Let us be imitators . . . ").

Greco-Roman lists, on the other hand, are less likely to use famous people in lists as models of behavior to imitate or avoid. They are more prone to use examples to prove or illustrate concepts without regard to the moral virtues of the people they list. The two exceptions appear to be Isocrates' argument for the validity of his own discipline of rhetoric, where he lists only orators from whom cities greatly benefitted (*Antidosis* 230-37), and Cicero's case for a broad, liberal education of orators (*De Or.* III.126-29; cf. III.132-36).

By contrast, in *Ad Philippum* 58-67 and *Archidamus* 40-48, Isocrates uses historical figures to prove points without regard for their virtue or vice. Alcidamas's list in Aristotle's *Rhetoric* II.23.11 presents examples of talented people who were honored, dwelling not on why they deserved the honor but upon why honor was given in spite of various restricting conditions. Likewise, in M. Aurelius III.3.1 the focus is on greatness without regard to virtue; and in VI. 47 he stresses diversity, again without reflection upon anything good in his examples that one should imitate. In the death-roll of Lucretius's *De Rer. Nat.* 1024-52, examples of goodness, military might, philosophical acumen, and inventive ability are all listed one after the other without effort to use them as models for imitation. Plutarch's *Amat.* 753D-54A rather humorously consists of negative examples which reveal how great men were manipulated and abused by poor women. And although *Amat.* 760C and 760E-62A deal with the great bravery exhibited by men because of love for their boy lovers, the argument of these lists is not affected by whether or not any particular person was or was not a virtuous model to imitate. Both the virtues and vices of those in *De Fortuna* (*Mor.* 97C-E) are given by Plutarch to illustrate that people chose both good and bad behavior and were not led blindly by Fate. Finally, the presence of hair on the heads of the men in Dio's humorous *Encomium on Hair* is hardly a matter of virtue.

Another difference between Greco-Roman and Jewish and Christian lists lies in the sources of well-known people. The Greco-Roman lists usually employ people from relatively recent and/or verifiable history, rarely appealing to stories from their sacred poets; whereas the Jewish and Christian lists typically draw examples from the sacred stories of the Old Testament. Aside from Homer's *Illiad* V.381-415, which is itself part of a sacred text, only Dio's spoof, *Encomium on Hair,* consists entirely of examples drawn from Greek or Roman sacred stories. Otherwise, Plutarch is somewhat unique in that he combines *exempla* from historical events, edifying tales and mythological stories in his lists in *Amatorius.*

All three of Isocrates' lists draw examples from verifiable history, conforming well to the advice of *Ad Alex.* 1439a1-3, that one should use examples ''that are nearest in time or place to our hearers, and if such are not available, such others as are most important and best known.'' Isocrates deals with important contemporary concerns of national defense in *Ad Philippum* and *Archidamus,* and he carefully choses historically verifiable *exempla* to argue his case. Also, in Isocrates' *Antidosis* 230-36 and Cicero's *De Oratore* III.126-29 and 132-35, well-known orators are selected as examples. Similar selection of figures from secular sources for use as *exempla* may be seen in Aristotle, *Rhetoric* II.23.11; Lucretius, *De Rer. Nat.* III.1024-52; M. Aurelius III.3.1; VI.47; and Plutarch, *De Fortuna (Mor.* 97C-E).

By contrast, Jewish and Christian lists employ few examples from outside the Old Testament. Philo's *Quis Rerum* 260-62 and *De Virt.* 198-227; Wisdom 10; 1 Maccabees 2:50-64; 4 Maccabees 18:10-19; 4 Ezra 7:106-11; and 1 Clement 9-12 and 17-18 all draw their examples exclusively from the Old Testament. CD II.14–IV.2 and 1 Clement 4-6, however, derive their *exempla* both from Old Testament stories and figures from more recent history. Composition of Jewish and Christian lists seems to indicate that their authors generally considered examples drawn from sacred stories to be more compelling as evidence than *exempla* from nonbiblical sources. This attitude differs from that reflected in the Greco-Roman lists whose authors by and large were hesitant to construct example lists from the stories of Homer and the other sacred poets.

Select Bibliography

Anderson, Charles P. "The Setting of the Epistle to the Hebrews." Ph.D. dissertation, Columbia University, 1969.

The Apocrypha and Pseudepigrapha of the Old Testament in English. Two volumes. Edited by R. H. Charles. Oxford: Clarendon Press, 1913.

The Apostolic Fathers. Volume 1. Translated by Kirsopp Lake. LCL. Cambridge: Harvard University Press, 1912.

Aristotle, *The "Art" of Rhetoric.* Translated by J. H. Freese, LCL. New York: G. P. Putnam's Sons, 1926.

Balogh, Josef. " 'Voces Paginarum': Beiträge zur Geschichte des lauten Lesens und Schreibens." *Philologus* 82 (1926): 84-109, 202-40.

Barrett, C. K. "The Eschatology of the Epistle to the Hebrews." In *The Background of the New Testament and its Eschatology,* 369-93. Edited by W. D. Davies and D. Daube. Cambridge: University Press, 1956.

Baumstark, A. "Anaphora." In Klauser (see below), 1:418-27.

Betz, Hans D. *Galatians.* Hermeneia. Philadelphia: Fortress Press, 1979.

Blass, F., and A. Debrunner. *A Greek Grammar of the New Testament and Other Early Christian Literature.* Translated and revised from the 9th and 10th editions by R. W. Funk. Chicago: University of Chicago Press, 1961.

Bleek, Friedrich. *Der Brief an die Hebräer*. Berlin: Ferdinand Dümmler, 1840.

Bligh, John. *Chiastic Analysis of the Epistle to the Hebrews*. Oxon, England: Heythrop College, 1966.

Bonner, Stanley F. *Education in Ancient Rome: From the elder Cato to the younger Pliny*. Berkeley: University of California Press, 1977.

Box, G. H. *The Ezra-Apocalypse*. London: Pitman & Sons, 1912.

Braun, H. "Das himmlische Vaterland bei Philo und im Hebräerbrief." In *Verborum Veritas*, Festschrift für G. Stahlin. Edited by O. Böcher and K. Haacker. Wuppertal: Brockhaus, 1970.

Breitenstein, Urs. *Beobachtungen zu Sprache, Stil und Gedankengut des Vierten Makkabäerbuchs*. Basel: Schwabe, 1976.

Bruce, A. B. *The Epistle to the Hebrews: The First Apology for Christianity*. Second edition. Edinburgh: T. & T. Clark, 1899.

Bruce, F. F. *The Epistle to the Hebrews*. NICNT. Grand Rapids: Eerdmans, 1964.

_____. "'To the Hebrews' or 'To the Essenes.'" *NTS* 9 (1963): 217-32.

Buchanan, George Wesley. *To the Hebrews*. The Anchor Bible. Garden City NY: Doubleday, 1972.

Büchsel, Friedrich. ἔλεγχος. In *TDNT* 2:473-76.

Buss, Martin J. "The Study of Forms." In *Old Testament Form Criticism*, Edited by John H. Hayes. San Antonio: Trinity University Press, 1974.

Calvin, John. *Commentaries on the Epistle of Paul the Apostle to the Hebrews*. Translated by J. Owen. Grand Rapids: Eerdmans, 1948.

Chaytor, H. J. *From Script to Print*. Cambridge: Cambridge University Press, 1945.

Cicero. *De Inventione* and *Topica*. Translated by H. M. Hubbell. LCL. Cambridge: Harvard University Press, 1949.

_____. *De Oratore*. Books I-III. Translated by E. W. Sutton. LCL. Cambridge: Harvard University Press, 1942.

Clark, Donald L. *Rhetoric in Greco-Roman Education*. New York: Columbia University Press, 1957.

Clark, Ernest G. *The Wisdom of Solomon*. The Cambridge Bible Commentary. Cambridge: University Press, 1973.

Collins, John J., and George W. E. Nickelsburg, editors. *Ideal Figures in Ancient Judaism: Profiles and Paradigms*. SBL Septuagint and Cognate Studies 12. Chico CA: Scholars Press, 1980.

The Communings with Himself of Marcus Aurelius Antoninus. Translated by C. R. Haines. LCL. New York: G. P. Putnam's Sons, 1916.

Crosby, Ruth. "Oral Delivery in the Middle Ages." *Speculum* 11 (1936): 88-110.

Culley, Robert C. *Oral-Formulaic Language in the Biblical Psalms*. Toronto: University of Toronto Press, 1967.

Dautzenberg, Gerhard. "Der Glaube im Hebräerbrief." *BibZeit* 17 (1973): 161-77.

D'Angelo, Mary R. *Moses in the Letter to the Hebrews*. SBL Dissertation Series 42. Missoula MT: Scholars Press, 1979.

Deissmann, Adolf. *Light from the Ancient East*. Translated by L. R. M. Strachan. New York: Doran, 1927.

Delitzsch, Franz. *Commentary on the Epistle to the Hebrews*. Two volumes. Clark's Foreign Theological Library 25. Translated by T. L. Kingsbury. Edinburgh: T. & T. Clark, 1870.

Delling, G. τελειόω. In *TDNT* 8:79-84.

Deutsch, Rosamund E. *The Pattern of Sound in Lucretius*. Published Dissertation. Bryn Mawr College, 1939.

Dey, Lala K. K. *The Intermediary World and Patterns of Perfection in Philo and Hebrews*. SBL Dissertation Series 25. Missoula MT: Scholars Press, 1975.

Dio Chrysostom. Volume 5. Translated by L. Crosby. LCL. Cambridge: Harvard University Press, 1932.

Eccles, Robert S. "The Purpose of the Hellenistic Patterns in the Epistle to the Hebrews." In *Religions in Antiquity: Essays in Memory of Erwin Ramsdell Goodenough*, 207-26. Edited by J. Neusner. Leiden: E. J. Brill, 1968.

Ellingworth, P. "Hebrews and 1 Clement: Literary Dependence or Common Tradition." *BibZeit* 23 (1979): 262-69.

Esbroeck, M. van. "Hébreux 11, 33-38 dans l'ancienne version géorgienne." *Biblica* 53 (1972): 43-64.

Farrington, B. "Form and Purpose in *De Rerum Natura*." In *Lucretius. Studies in Latin Literature and its Influence*. Edited by D. R. Dudley. London: Routledge & Kegan Paul, 1965.

Feld, Helmut. *Martin Luthers und Wendelin Steinbachs Vorlesungen über den Hebräerbrief: Eine Studie zur Geschichte der neutestamentlichen Exegese und Theologie*. Wiesbaden: Franz Steiner, 1971.

Foley, John M., editor. *Oral Traditional Literature: A Festschrift for Albert Bates Lord.* Columbus OH: Slavica Press, 1981.

Gouge, William. *Commentary on Hebrews.* Edinburgh: J. Nichol, 1866. Reprint. Grand Rapids: Kregel Publications, 1980.

Graber, Friedrich. *Der Glaubensweg des Volkes Gottes. Ein Erklärung von Hebräer 11 als Beitrag zum Verständnis des Alten Testamentes.* Zurich: Zwingli, 1943.

Grant, R. M., and H. H. Graham. *The Apostolic Fathers.* Volume 2. New York: Thomas Nelson and Sons, 1965.

Grässer, Erich. *Der Glaube im Hebräerbrief.* Marburger Theologische Studien 2. Marburg: N. G. Elwert, 1965.

Gyllenberg, R. "Die Komposition des Hebräerbriefs." *Svensk Exegetisk Årsbok* 22-23 (1957–58): 137-47.

Hadas, Moses. *Ancilla to Classical Reading.* New York: Columbia University Press, 1954.

Hagen, Kenneth. *Hebrews Commenting from Erasmus to Bèze: 1516–1598.* Beiträge zur Geschichte der Biblischen Exegese 23. Tübingen: J. C. B. Mohr, 1981.

Hagner, Donald A. *The Use of the Old and New Testaments in Clement of Rome.* Leiden: E. J. Brill, 1973.

Havelock, Eric A. "The Ancient Art of Oral Poetry." *Philosophy and Rhetoric* 19 (1979): 187-202.

Havelock, Eric A., and Jackson P. Herschell, editors. *Communication Arts in the Ancient World.* New York: Hastings House, 1978.

Haymes, Edward R. *A Bibliography of Studies Relating to Parry's and Lord's Oral Theory.* Publications of the Milman Parry Collection: Documentation and Planning Series 1. Cambridge: Harvard University Press, 1973. (More than 500 entries.)

Heller, Jan. "Stabesanbetung? [Hebr. 11, 21-Gen. 47, 31]." *Communio Viatorum.* 16 (1973): 257-65.

Héring, Jean. *The Epistle to the Hebrews.* Translated by A. W. Heathcote and P. J. Allcock. London: Epworth Press, 1970.

Hofius, Otfried. *Katapausis: Die Vorstellung vom endzeitlichen Ruheort im Hebräerbrief.* Wissenschaftliche Untersuchung en zum Neuen Testament 11. Tübingen: J. C. B. Mohr, 1970.

_____. *"Stomata machaires* Hebr 11:34.*"* Hebr. 11:34.*" ZNW* 62 (1971): 129-30.

Holoka, James P. "Homeric Originality: A Survey." *Classical World* 66 (1973): 257-93. Annotated bibliography with 214 entries.

Homer, *The Iliad.* Translated by A. T. Murray. LCL. New York: G. P. Putnam's Sons, 1924.

Hubert, Martin, Jr. "Amatorius *(Moralia* 748E-771E)." In *Plutarch's Ethical Writings and Early Christian Literature*, 442-537. Studia ad Corpus Hellenisticum Novi Testamenti 4. Edited by Hans D. Betz. Leiden: E. J. Brill, 1978.

Hughes, Philip E. "The Doctrine of Creation in Hebrews 11:3." *Biblical Theology Bulletin* 2 (1972): 64-77.

Isocrates. Two volumes. Translated by G. Norlin. LCL. New York: G. P. Putnam's Sons, 1928.

Johnsson, W. G. "The Pilgrimage Motif in the Book of Hebrews." *JBL* 97 (1978): 239-51.

Jones, P. R. "The Figure of Moses as a Heuristic Device for Understanding the Pastoral Intent of Hebrews." *RevExp* 76 (1979): 95-107.

Jost, Karl. *Das Beispiel und Vorbild der Vorfahren bei den attischen Rednern und Geschichtschreibern bei Demosthenes.* Regensburg: Michael Lassleben, 1935.

Käsemann, Ernst. *Das wandernde Gottesvolk: Eine Untersuchung zum Hebräerbrief.* Göttingen: Vandenhoeck & Ruprecht, 1959.

Kelber, Werner. "Mark and Oral Tradition." *Semeia* 16 (1980): 7-55.

_____. *The Oral and the Written Gospel. The Hermeneutics of Speaking and Writing in the Synoptic Tradition, Mark, Paul, and Q.* Philadelphia: Fortress Press, 1983.

Kennedy, George A. *Classical Rhetoric and Its Christian and Secular Tradition from Ancient to Modern Times.* Chapel Hill: University of North Carolina Press, 1980.

_____. *New Testament Interpretation Through Rhetorical Criticism.* Chapel Hill: The University of North Carolina Press, 1984.

_____. *The Art of Persuasion in Greece.* Princeton: Princeton University Press, 1963.

Kessler, Martin. "A Methodological Setting for Rhetorical Criticism." In *Art and Meaning: Rhetoric in Biblical Literature*, 1-19. Edited by D. J. A. Clines, et al. JSOT Supplement Series 19. Sheffield: JSOT Press, 1982.

Kirk, G. S. *Homer and the Oral Tradition*. Cambridge: University Press, 1976.

Klauser, Theodor, editor. *Reallexicon für Antike und Christentum: Sachwörterbuch zur Auseinandersetzung des Christentums mit der Antiken Welt*. Eleven volumes. Stuttgart: Hiersemann, 1950–1981.

Koester, Helmut. ὑπόστασις. In *TDNT* 8:572-89.

Lake, Kirsopp. *The Apostolic Fathers*. Volume 1. LCL. Cambridge: Harvard University Press, 1912.

Lausberg, Heinrich. *Handbuch der literarischen Rhetorik: Eine Grundlegung der Literaturwissenschaft*. München: Max Hueber, 1960.

Lee, Thomas R. "Studies in the Form of Sirach (Ecclesiasticus) 44-50." Ph.D. dissertation, Graduate Theological Union, Berkeley, 1979.

Lewis, Thomas W., III. "The Theological Logic in Hebrews 10:19-12:29 and the Appropriation of the Old Testament." Ph.D. dissertation, Drew University, 1964.

Liddell, Henry G. and Scott, Robert. *A Greek-English Lexicon*. Ninth edition. Revised by H. S. Jones. Oxford: Clarendon Press, 1940.

Lightfoot, J. B. *S. Clement of Rome: The Two Epistles to the Corinthians*. London: Macmillan, 1869.

_____. *The Apostolic Fathers*. Volume 2. London: Macmillan, 1890.

Lohmann, Dieter. *Die Komposition der Reden in der Ilias*. Untersuchungen zur antiken Literatur und Geschichte. Band 6. Berlin: Walter de Gruyter & Co., 1970.

Lucretius. *De Rerum Natura*. Translated by W. H. D. Rouse. LCL. New York: G. P. Putnam's Sons, 1924.

_____. *De Rerum Natura. Book III*. Edited by E. J. Kenney. Cambridge: University Press, 1971.

Lührmann, Dieter. "Henoch und die Metanoia." *ZNW* 66 (1975): 103-16.

Marrou, Henri-I. *A History of Education in Antiquity*. Translated by G. Lamb. London: Sheed and Ward, 1956.

Martin, Hubert, "Amatoris." In *Plutarch's Ethical Writings and Early Christian Literature*. Edited by H. D. Betz. Leiden: E. J. Brill, 1978.

Martin, Josef. *Antike Rhetorik: Technik und Methode*. Handbuch der Altertumswissenschaft. München: C. H. Beck, 1974.

McCown, Wayne G. "Ὁ ΛΟΓΟΣ ΤΗΕ ΠΑΡΑΚΛΗΣΕΩΣ, The Nature and Function of the Hortatory Sections in the Epistle to the Hebrews." Th.D. dissertation, Union Theological Seminary, Richmond, 1970.

McCullough, J. C. "Some Recent Developments in Research on the Epistle to the Hebrews." *Irish Biblical Studies* 2 (1980): 141-65.

_____. "The Old Testament Quotations in Hebrews." *NTS* 26 (1980): 363-79.

Meeks, Wayne A. "Moses as God and King." In *Religions in Antiquity: Essays in Memory of Erwin Ramsdell Goodenough*, 354-71. Edited by J. Neusner. Leiden: E. J. Brill, 1968.

Metzger, Bruce M. *A Textual Commentary on the Greek New Testament.* London and New York: United Bible Societies, 1971.

Michel, Otto. *Der Brief an die Hebräer.* Thirteenth edition. Meyer Kommentar. Göttingen: Vandenhoeck & Ruprecht, 1975.

Moffatt, James. *A Critical and Exegetical Commentary on the Epistle to the Hebrews.* ICC. New York: Charles Scribner's Sons, 1924.

Montefiore, Hugh. *A Commentary on the Epistle to the Hebrews.* Harper's NT Commentaries. New York: Harper & Row, 1964.

Muilenberg, James. "Form Criticism and Beyond." *JBL* 88 (1969): 1-18.

Mussies, G. *Dio Chrysostom and the New Testament.* Studia ad Corpus Hellenisticum Novi Testamenti 2. Leiden: E. J. Brill, 1972.

Nelson, William. "From 'Listen, Lordings' to 'Dear Reader.'" *University of Toronto Quarterly* 46 (1976–1977): 111-24.

Neuhaus, G. O. *Studien zu den poetischen Stucken im 1. Makkabaerbuch.* Forschung zur Bibel. Wurzburg: Echter, 1974.

Norden, E. *Agnostos Theos.* 5. Auflage. Darmstadt: Wissenschaftliche Buchgesellschaft, 1971.

O'Connor, Michael P. *Hebrew Verse Structure.* Winona Lake IN: Eisenbrauns, 1980.

Oehler, Robert. *Mythologische Exempla in der älteren griechischen Dichtung.* Basel: H. R. Sauerlander & Co., 1925.

Ong, Walter J. *Orality and Literacy: The Technologizing of the Word.* New York: Methuen, 1982.

Owen, John. *An Exposition of the Epistle to the Hebrews.* Volume 7. New York: Robert Carter & Brothers, 1855.

Parry, Milman. *The Making of Homeric Verse: The Collected Papers of Milman Parry.* Edited by Adam Parry. Oxford: Clarendon Press, 1971.

Perelman, Chaim, and L. Olbrechts-Tyteca. *The New Rhetoric: A Treatise on Argumentation.* Translated by J. Wilkinson and P. Weaver. Notre Dame: University of Notre Dame Press, 1969.

Peterson, David. *Hebrews and Perfection: An Examination of the Concept of Perfection in the "Epistle to the Hebrews."* Society for NT Studies Monograph Series 47. Cambridge: Cambridge University Press, 1982.

Philo. Volumes 4, 8. Translated by F. H. Colson. LCL. Cambridge: Harvard University Press, 1929.

Plutarch. *Moralia.* Volume 9. Translated by E. L. Minar, Jr., et al. LCL. Cambridge: Harvard University Press, 1927.

Polybius. *The Histories.* Volume 3. Translated by W. R. Paton, LCL. Cambridge: Harvard University Press, 1923.

Price, Bennett J. "*Paradeigma* and *Exemplum* in Ancient Rhetorical Theory." Ph.D. dissertation, University of California at Berkeley, 1975.

Quintilian. *Institutio Oratoria.* Four volumes. Translated by H. E. Butler. LCL. New York: G. P. Putnam's Sons, 1921.

Reese, J. M. "Plan and Structure in the Book of Wisdom." *CBQ* 27 (1965): 391-99.

Reid, Richard. "The Use of the Old Testament in the Epistle to the Hebrews." Th.D. dissertation, Union Theological Seminary, New York, 1964.

Rhetorica ad Alexandrum. Translated by H. Rackham. LCL. Cambridge: Harvard University Press, 1936.

Rhetorica ad Herennium. Translated by Harry Caplan. LCL. Cambridge: Harvard University Press, 1937.

Russell, D. A. *Criticism in Antiquity.* Berkeley: University of California Press, 1981.

Sampson, Francis, S. *A Critical and Exegetical Commentary on the Epistle to the Hebrews.* Edited by R. L. Dabney. New York: Robert Carter & Brothers, 1856.

Sanders, Louis. *L'hellénisme de Sainte Clément de Rome et le paulinisme.* Studia Hellenistica. Louvaine: Bibliotheca Universitatis, 1943.

Schille, Gottfried. "Katechese und Taufliturgie: Erwägungen zu Hbr 11." *ZNW* 51 (1960): 112-31.

Schmitt, Von Armin. "Struktur, Herkunft und Bedeutung der Beispielreihe in Weish 10." *BibZeit* 21 (1977): 1-22.

Scott, E. F. *The Epistle to the Hebrews: Its Doctrine and Significance*. Edinburgh: T. & T. Clark, 1922.

Septuaginta. Edited by A. Rahlfs. Stuttgart: Deutsche Bibelstiftung, 1935.

Skehan, P. W. "The Text and Structure of the Book of Wisdom." *Traditio* 3 (1945): 1-12.

Smith, Jerome. *A Priest Forever: A Study of Typology and Eschatology in Hebrews*. London: Sheed and Ward, 1969.

Snyder, Jane M. *Puns and Poetry in Lucretius' De Rerum Natura*. Amsterdam: B. R. Gruner, 1980.

Spicq, C. *L'Épître aux Hébreux*. Two volumes. Études Bibliques. Paris: Librairie Lecoffre, 1952–1953.

Stolz, Benjamin A. and Shannon, Richard S., editors. *Oral Literature and the Formula*. Ann Arbor: Center for the Coordination of Ancient and Modern Studies, 1976.

Strack, Hermann L., and Paul Billerbeck. *Die Briefe des Neuen Testaments und die Offenbarung Johannis*. Kommentar zum Neuen Testament aus Talmud und Midrasch 3. München: C. H. Beck, 1926.

Stuart, Moses. *A Commentary on the Epistle to the Hebrews*. Second edition. New York: J. Leavitt, 1833.

Swetnam, James. "Form and Content in Hebrews 1-6." *Biblica* 53 (1972): 368-85.

_____. "Form and Content in Hebrews 7-13." *Biblica* 55 (1974): 333-48.

_____. "On the Literary Genre of the 'Epistle' to the Hebrews." *NovTest* 11 (1969): 261-69.

Swete, Henry B. *An Introduction to the Old Testament in Greek*. Revised edition. Cambridge: Cambridge University Press, 1914.

Tholuck, A. *A Commentary on the Epistle to the Hebrews*. Two volumes. The Biblical Cabinet 39. Translated by J. Hamilton. Edinburgh: Thomas Clark, 1842.

Thompson, A. L. *Responsibility for Evil in the Theodicy of IV Ezra*. SBL Dissertation Series 29. Missoula MT: Scholars Press, 1977.

Thompson, James W. "'That Which Abides': Some Metaphysical Assumptions in the Epistle to the Hebrews." Ph.D. dissertation, Vanderbilt University, Nashville, 1974.

_____. *The Beginnings of Christian Philosophy: The Epistle to the Hebrews.* CBQMS 13. Washington DC: The Catholic Biblical Association of America, 1982.

_____. "The Underlying Unity of Hebrews." *Restoration Quarterly* 18 (1975): 129-36.

Thurén, Jukka. *Das Lobopfer der Hebräer.* Studien zum Aufbau und Anliegen von Hebräerbrief 13. Acta Academiae Aboensis, series A, volume 47, number 1. Åbo, 1973.

Thyen, Hartwig. *Der Stil der Jüdisch-Hellenistischen Homilie.* Forschungen zur Religion und Literatur des Alten und Neuen Testaments 47. Göttingen: Vandenhoeck & Ruprecht, 1955.

Titi Lucreti Cari De Rerum Natura. Volume 2. Edited by C. Bailey. Oxford: Clarendon Press, 1947.

Towner, Wayne S. *The Rabbinic "Enumeration of Scriptural Examples": A Study of a Rabbinic Pattern of Discourse with Special Reference to Mekhilta D'R. Ishmael.* Studia Post-Biblica. Leiden: E. J. Brill, 1973.

Turner, Nigel. *A Grammar of New Testament Greek.* Volume 4, *Style.* Edinburgh: T. & T. Clark, 1976.

Tymeson, Gale E. "The Material World in Gnosticism and the Epistle to the Hebrews." Ph.D. dissertation, University of Pittsburgh, 1975.

Vaganay, L. "Le plan de l'Épître aux Hébreux." In *Memorial Lagrange,* 269-77. Edited by L.-H. Vincent. Paris, 1940.

Vanhoye, Albert. "Discussions sur la structure de l'Épître aux Hébreux." *Biblica* 55 (1974): 349-80.

_____. *La Structure Littéraire de L'Épître aux Hébreux.* Studia Neotestamentica 1. Paris: Desclée De Brouwer, 1963.

Wallach, Barbara P. *Lucretius and the Diatribe against the Fear of Death: De Rerum Natura III 830-1094.* Mnemosyne Bibliotheca Classica Batava. Leiden: E. J. Brill, 1976.

Wendland, Paul. *Die urchristlichen Literaturformen.* Tübingen: J. C. B. Mohr, 1912.

Westcott, B. F. *The Epistle to the Hebrews.* London: Macmillan, 1903.

Wetstein, Johann Jacob. ʽΗ ΚΑΙΝΗ ΔΙΑΘΗΚΗ, *Novum Testamentum Grae-cum: Nec Non Commentario Pleniore Ex Scriptoribus Veteribus Hebraeis, Graecis et Latinis.* Tomus 2. Amsterdam: Ex Officina Dommeriana, 1752.

Willcock, M. M. *A Commentary on Homer's Iliad: Books I-VI.* London: Mac-millan, 1970.

Williamson, Ronald. *Philo and the Epistle to the Hebrews.* Arbeiten zur Literatur und Geschichte des hellenistischen Judentums 4. Leiden: E. J. Brill, 1970.

Windisch, Hans. *Der Hebräerbrief.* Zweite Auflage. Handbuch zum Neuen Tes-tament 14. Tübingen: J. C. B. Mohr, 1931.

Winston, David. *The Wisdom of Solomon.* Anchor Bible 43. Garden City NY: Doubleday, 1979.

Wright, A. G. "The Structure of the Book of Wisdom." *Biblica* 48 (1967): 165-84.

_____. "The Structure of Wisd. 11-19." *CBQ* 27 (1965): 28-34.

The Zadokite Documents. Second edition. Translated by Chaim Rabin. Oxford: Clarendon Press, 1958.

Zerwick, Maximillan. *Biblical Greek.* Translated by J. Smith. Rome: Scripta Pontificii Instituti Biblici, 1963.

Zoll, Gallus. *Cicero Platonis Aemulus: Untersuchung über die Form von Ciceros Dialogen, besonders von De Oratore.* Zurich: Juris, 1962.

Zuntz, Günther. *The Text of the Epistles.* London: Oxford University Press, 1953.

Indexes

Author Index

Scripture Index

Old Testament

New Testament

Jewish Sources Outside the Canon

Christian Sources Outside the Canon

Greek and Roman Sources

Topical Index

Abel, 25, 42, 45, 71, 107
Abraham, 18, 21, 42, 43, 44, 45, 47, 48, 52, 67, 82, 83, 84
adjunction, 54, 66, 70
Aesop, 94, 104
Alexander, 51
Alcibiades, 20
amplification, 40
analogy, 95
anaphora, 3, 19, 41, 42, 48, 49, 50, 51, 52, 55, 57, 65, 68, 71
anaphoric, 21, 23, 24, 25, 41, 46, 48, 50, 53, 55, 57, 65, 91
Anaxagoras, 66
antithesis, 31, 40, 63, 75, 78, 79, 80, 81
antonomasia, 83, 84
Aphrodite, 49
apostasy, 65, 87
Ares, 50
Aristeides, 51
asyndeton, 52, 60, 61, 62, 64, 65, 68, 69, 82, 91
Barak, 21, 57, 58
Beispielreihen, 10, 12, 13
Beza, 34
cadence, 22, 31
Cain, 42, 107
chiasm, 91
chiastic, 62
Chilon, 66
Christ, 76, 77, 78, 87, 89
Christian, 2, 3, 4, 10, 11, 13, 18, 20, 39, 65, 72, 80, 87, 89, 91, 107, 108, 109

circumlocution, 81, 82, 83, 84
collatio, 101
colon, 60
comma, 61
Conon, 20
contentio, 75
Crassus, 54, 99, 101, 105
creatio ex nihilo, 26
David, 18, 21, 57, 58, 67
deductive, 95, 96, 97, 102, 105
deliberative, 94
Democritus, 71
diatribe, 11
Diomedes, 49
Dione, 50
Egypt, 46, 47, 76, 77, 78, 89
Elijah, 67
Enoch, 25, 45, 71
enthymeme, 95, 96, 100
epideictic, 94
epithet, 83
exempla, 13, 93, 94, 96, 98, 99, 100, 101, 102, 103, 104, 105, 109
Exhortatio, 5
Exordium, 5
fable, 94
Fate, 51
forensic, 94
form criticism, 8, 9
Gattung, 9
genre, 8, 9, 11
Gideon, 21, 57, 58, 59
Gracchus, 99

DATE DUE

OCT 1 3 '89		
DEC 1 9 '89		
DEC 1 8 1996		
APR 3 0 2001		